# · A HISTORY LOVER'S ·
## GUIDE TO

# ALBUQUERQUE

# · A HISTORY LOVER'S ·
## GUIDE TO
# ALBUQUERQUE

ROGER M. ZIMMERMAN

THE
History
PRESS

Published by The History Press
Charleston, SC
www.historypress.com

Copyright © 2019 by Roger Zimmerman
All rights reserved

First published 2019

Manufactured in the United States

ISBN 9781467142052

Library of Congress Control Number: 2019945090

*I dedicate this book to the Albuquerque Historical Society,*
*as it was this organization that showed the enthusiasm for and dedication to*
*history that stimulated me to be an active history lover.*

# CONTENTS

# PREFACE

This book is about the long and unique history of Albuquerque, New Mexico. Albuquerque was founded in 1706 within the Native American province of Tiguex, which became located within the Spanish province of Santa Fe de Nuevo México. The Villa of Alburquerque (later Albuquerque) was located at the edge of a monstrous geological fault that had a five-mile vertical separation in layers of rock. A more than one-thousand-year-old change in the course of the Rio Grande created a seventeen-square-mile floodplain that became the eventual site of downtown Albuquerque. Native Americans had settled in and around the floodplain and created rudimentary irrigation practices. Spanish explorers came with advanced weaponry in 1540, and conflicts between the visitors and indigenous population developed. The sustained immigration of Spanish settlers led to continued tension, serious conflicts and a major province-wide pueblo revolt and eventual resolution. Spanish descendants and the Tiwa-speaking Pueblo Indians have coexisted peacefully since. Trade opportunities with the United States developed when Mexico separated from Spain in 1821 and economic activities increased when the United States took over the region twenty-five years later. The growth of Albuquerque in the Territory of New Mexico and later state was significantly influenced by the coming of the AT&SF Railway, the growth of highway transportation over Routes 85 and 66 and then World War II. Albuquerque became a focal point in the development of the atomic age during and after that serious conflict.

# PREFACE

It is hoped that the reader will find this information interesting and that it will make it easy to understand the underlying historical nuances that have contributed to our history. It is intended that this guide will help the reader find satisfaction in either visiting or exploring topics of choice.

# ACKNOWLEDGEMENTS

The author is indebted to many for helping produce this book. This book wouldn't have even been attempted without knowledge of the works of Marc Simmons. Marc produced a very thorough and detailed book about a narrative history of Albuquerque through the 1970s. A bibliography is provided, but it should be realized that Simmons's works form the factual basis for most of the information in this guidebook.

Many people provided valuable contributions and are gratefully thanked. Norman Falk provided many photographs and valuable advice in reviewing various drafts. My eldest son, Paul, provided valuable computer support, thoughtful reviews and very useful maps. Diane Schaller and Richard Ruddy, from Historic Albuquerque Inc., provided many photographs and support in the preparation of the book. They were the instructors who spent two years training downtown tour guides. They were enthusiastic supporters of what I was trying to accomplish. Albuquerque Historical Society (AHS) board members Peter Ives and Secretary Joe Sabatini offered very helpful advice and suggestions for the text. AHS board members Roland Penttila and Susan Schwartz provided valuable photographic assistance. AHS president (2008–13), vice-president (2013–19) and incoming president (for 2019) Janet Saiers and treasurer Dan Jones have been very supportive in getting the project going and will be most helpful when the book is on the market. AHS member Dave Furbush is thanked for providing a very informative tour of Old Town.

# ACKNOWLEDGEMENTS

There are many outside the society who have been very helpful in obtaining the images. Jill Hartke (Albuquerque Museum), Portia Vescio (Center for Southwest Research) and Troy Rummler (Sandia National Laboratories) provided multiple images. Individual images came from Caitlin Cano (Indian Pueblo Cultural Center), Kindsey Cooper (National Hispanic Cultural Center), Jennifer Hayden (National Nuclear Museum), Dale Kissner (Petroglyph National Monument), Mary Beth Hermans (Maxwell Museum), Debra Novak (Natural History Museum), Raquel Waters (MRGCD), Marilee Schmidt Nason (Balloon Museum) and Jessie Perkins (KAFB Public Affairs). Doug Lutz (Sunport Public Affairs) is thanked for his helpful background information on the development of the airport.

# INTRODUCTION

**A**lbuquerque is the largest city in the state of New Mexico. It has a unique history and setting that makes it a very special place as a history lover's paradise. This story starts on top of Sandia Peak, which is located on the east side of the city. A view from the top of the mountain toward the southwest shows a city that is a treasure to all who travel—by auto, tramway or foot—to the top of the peak. The peak is 10,678 feet above sea level. The view that is seen is in the neighborhood of 5,000 feet below the peak. This means that the viewer is looking down over a mile in elevation to a relatively flat area that is covered, for the most part, with buildings. The flat area is part of the Middle Valley of the Rio Grande. It was the location of villages and agricultural fields for the early Native American residents.

The geologic setting for Albuquerque is unique and has much to do with our history. More than 10 million years ago, the area containing these buildings was originally part of relatively flat terrain. There were some low hills and plains that marked the terrain. Slowly, pressures in Earth's crust created a rift in the Rio Grande Valley, and in the process, a block of metamorphic rock and underlying granite rose up from formations located far underground. The place where the Sandia Crest photograph was taken was at one time about three miles lower in elevation—a block of rock nearly twenty miles long was pushed up in a tilted configuration. The west side of the mountains shows the rough fault exposure of the granite and is colorful at sunsets. The eastern side of the mountains is somewhat of a plain surface

Westerly View of Albuquerque from Sandia Peak Crest. *Norman Falk, photographer.*

that dips severely down. There is a ski area on it. Metamorphic rock is evident on the crest and east side of the mountain, and the surface is covered with trees. The mountain is called Sandia, which in Spanish means watermelon. The exposed west face shows red at sunset, and the east side is green; the combination of both forms an image similar to a broken watermelon, which makes the name quite appropriate. A fossil-studded layer of limestone is part of metamorphic rock deposits. In effect, you can go to the top of the Sandia Mountain to find remains from an ancient lakebed. What an amazing natural phenomenon.

The flat area in the center of the view from Sandia Peak has a complex and unique history. After the Sandia block rose, the land immediately to the west dropped nearly two miles down and a depression resulted, which is called the Rio Grande Trough. The trough, which is about twenty-five miles wide and about eighty-five miles long, forms the underlying strata for the region between north of Bernalillo and Belen. Essentially, the trough is the region between the Sandia Mountains and the Rio Puerco to the west. The Pennsylvanian formation located at the crest is now about twenty-six thousand feet higher than the matching formation in the trough. There was a five-mile separation in this geologic layer that occurred over geologic time.

Without getting too deep into geology, it is important to recognize that these landmass actions are part of the Rio Grande Rift. The rift is a major fault in the continental plate that underlies North America. The rift extends from central Colorado to Chihuahua in Mexico. The Rio Grande follows the rift from southern Colorado to El Paso, Texas, and the Sandia Mountain uplifting and Rio Grande Trough displacements are part of it.

Over time, the trough has filled back up with sand, gravel, silt, clay and water from the nearby highlands. On the west side of the trough is another fault zone where volcanoes and igneous intrusions are evident. Two fractures in Earth's surface developed, and five volcanic cones, prominent on the west mesa, rest on a platform of black rock that was laid down in successive eruptions some 190,000 years ago. All of these actions contributed to the filling in of the ten-thousand-foot-deep trough.

Several areas can be identified from the peak. The dark area going from right to left is the bosque (forest) area of primarily cottonwood trees around the Rio Grande. A neighborhood of Alameda, which was once a pueblo, is located immediately behind the top of the Douglas fir tree in the view. The Sandia Pueblo Indian Reservation is located in the open space to the right of the tree. The reservation forms the northeastern boundary for Albuquerque. Acquired buffalo roam in the open fields on the Sandia Reservation.

The Rio Grande is the major drainage river for the Rio Grande Rift and, as a result, has been the major driver for changes occurring in the basin. This was an untamed river that had no dams or relief from flooding in the early days. The 1,200-mile-long river flows from the headwaters in southwest Colorado down through New Mexico to form the international boundary with Mexico and finally drains into the Gulf of Mexico.

The relatively flat area shown in the view to the southwest was severely impacted by a change in the alignment of the Rio Grande some one to two thousand years ago. Downtown Albuquerque is located in a floodplain that existed between the old and new channels, and this is shown on a map, seen on the following page.

The map shows the major areas that are discussed in this book. The original river went generally along a line between the Alameda and Barelas neighborhoods. US Highway 85 gives a good indication of where the original channel was. The railroad tracks are just east of the original channel. The deviation forming the curved part of the river lengthened the course of the river slightly and created about seventeen square miles of floodplain.

Periodic flooding by the Rio Grande on the filled-in trough resulted in two problems. First, many times the flooding was destructive. Second, the

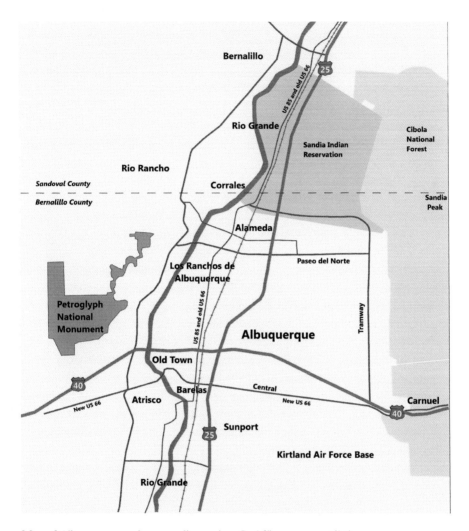

Map of Albuquerque and surrounding region. *Paul Zimmerman compilation.*

flooding brought about severe drainage problems. At the time of the city's founding, the water table lay very close to the surface. There were ponds and swamps in the region between Alameda and Barelas. Control of the surface and subsurface water was essential if the community was to grow.

This guide also covers immigration-related changes induced to the Albuquerque region by humans that have occurred over the period from fifty to nearly five hundred years ago. Watershed events have occurred since the settlement of the Tiwa-speaking Native Americans in the 1300s. These will be briefly introduced, and more information and explanations will be provided throughout the book.

The indigenous Tiwa-speaking Indians moved into the high ground in the region seen in the Sandia Peak view mostly between Alameda and Bernalillo. They also settled some fourteen to fifteen miles south in Isleta Pueblo, which was located on high ground as well. There were more than a dozen villages in what was called by Francisco Vásquez de Coronado the Province of Tiguex.

The first encounter of the Tiwa Indians with Spanish explorers occurred in 1540. The Coronado expedition chose to winter in the region between Sandia Pueblo and Bernalillo at a site that was eleven to twelve miles north of downtown Albuquerque. The explorers and the Native American residents ended up in conflict as they tried to share limited resources. This is known as the Tiguex War. Tiwa residents were chased from their villages when Coronado was in the region. These conflicts set the stage for future Native American–Spanish interactions.

The next major event was the colonization of the region by the Spanish government. The region was organized in 1598 as the Province of Santa Fe de Nuevo México with Juan de Oñate y Salazar as the first governor. A feature in the formation of the province was the establishment of El Camino Real de Tierra Adentro (the Royal Road of the Interior Land), a route running 1,600 miles from Mexico City to Santa Fe. The road brought settlers, goods and information to the province and carried crops, livestock and crafts to the markets in New Spain (later Mexico).

Oñate had difficulties interfacing with the existing populations, particularly in Acoma, and left the area in 1606 under an administrative censure. His successor, Don Pedro de Peralta, came to the task with the goal to organize the natives and convert them to Christianity so they would be good Spanish citizens. The Spanish clergy wanted the natives to accept pure Christian practices and did not have any tolerance for native customs or practices. Also, the Spanish used the natives as forced laborers, as they built churches at most of the pueblos.

Opposition to the occupation practices flared up in 1680, when the Pueblos under Tewa leaders banded together to oust the Spanish from the region. In the Pueblo Revolt of 1680, the natives were successful in chasing the Spanish out of the Province of Santa Fe de Nuevo México. The roles and effects of the revolt on the local Tiwa Pueblos are discussed in this work.

The Spanish came back in 1692 with three goals. One was Christianizing the natives, with tolerance for native customs and practices. Another was

# INTRODUCTION

Spain's recognition of Pueblo ownership of Indian lands; vacant land between Indian lands would be granted to Spanish settlers. Finally, the Spanish would not compel natives into forced labor situations. These goals were accepted by the Pueblos. In effect, the Spanish and the Native Americans were seeking ways to coexist.

The initial townsite for Albuquerque, called Old Town Albuquerque, was founded on the unique floodplain of the Rio Grande in 1706. The original site was located on ground in the floodplain some three to four feet higher. The Villa de Alburquerque (the spelling will be explained) was founded by short-term Spanish governor Don Francisco de Cuervo y Valdéz, who selected the floodplain over higher ground at Bernalillo in a controversial decision. Residents from Bernalillo became the first settlers to the new villa.

The next major event was the changing of the ownership of the Province of Santa Fe de Nuevo México from Spain to the newly formed Mexico in 1821. Governmental regulations didn't change radically, but there was one major difference that affected the citizens in the province. Mexico encouraged trade with the United States, while Spain had strictly prohibited it. Trade goods could come and go from Independence, Missouri, over the newly formed Santa Fe Trail or from Chihuahua, Mexico, on El Camino Real. Albuquerque blossomed, as it was the breadbasket for the traders. Crops, cattle and sheep were raised in the floodplain, and trade on the trails flourished.

Residents of Albuquerque welcomed the U.S. Army in 1846 with the chance to gain American citizenship. After the final settlement of the Treaty of Guadalupe Hidalgo and later Compromise of 1850, most of the old Santa Fe de Nuevo México province would become the U.S. territory of New Mexico. One of the features of the change in governments was that the United States took on the task of protecting traders on both trails from raiding Native American tribes. Forts were built. There was a brief interlude in 1862 when the Confederate army occupied Albuquerque for about six weeks. There was even the inconsequential Battle of Albuquerque, which will be discussed. Replicas of two Confederate cannons are displayed on the Old Town Plaza as a testament to this action.

The next major event occurred with the arrival of the railroad in 1880. Bernalillo was the preferred candidate for the depot, but it was dropped from contention. Promoters in Albuquerque were successful in acquiring the depot and supporting railyards, and New Town Albuquerque emerged as a new community to complement the existing Old Town. New Town residents had the desire to build a thriving community and succeeded due to early growth initiatives in New Town and a stimulus from a growing Protestant population.

The invention of the automobile brought about an increased growth in the community and a major change in the physical configuration of Albuquerque. In 1926, US 85 was established as a north–south highway in New Mexico and was generally aligned with El Camino Real. US 66 was also established and coexisted with US 85 from Las Vegas, New Mexico, to Los Lunas, New Mexico. State and federal officials decided to realign US 66 in 1931, and this was finalized in 1937. The realigned US 66, which saved 107 miles of interstate travel, went east–west along the major thoroughfare of Central Avenue (formerly Railroad Avenue). Growth along the east–west axis dominated the development of the city, and Albuquerque changed from being a linear north–south city to a bi-linear city.

The last major event that will be discussed is the impact of World War II on the community. In 1939, the city and U.S. Army agreed to share runways at the new airport on the east mesa. World War II arrived, and the highly secret Manhattan Project, which was to produce the first atomic weapon, was located at nearby Los Alamos. Albuquerque became the highway, rail and air center for the project. At the end of the war, the U.S. government decided to use Albuquerque to provide hardware designs and developments and implementation of delivery capabilities for our nation's nuclear forces as part of Cold War activities.

New Town Albuquerque grew through the assimilation of diverse ethnic and religious populations. Statues, plaques, cemeteries and murals emerged to highlight these activities. Museums, libraries, educational facilities, churches, parks and recreational areas grew as expected. Special and unique treasures—like the establishment of Petroglyph National Monument in the city limits, the world-renowned growth of the sport of ballooning, the addition of the Sandia Peak Tramway or the emergence of the Unser family in automobile racing—are briefly highlighted to prove that this area is a history lover's paradise.

The following chapters will provide additional details regarding these events so the reader can appreciate the unique and enchanting happenings that have created strong emotional attachments to what researchers of the past have uncovered.

# PROVINCE OF TIGUEX

**N**ative Americans who spoke the Tiwa language were living in some twelve to sixteen villages along the Rio Grande between what is now Bernalillo, New Mexico, to the north and Isleta Pueblo to the south. Archaeologists think there were more villages, but definitive evidence is difficult to find. This is a north–south distance of about thirty miles for the province. Coronado, in his visit to New Mexico in 1540–42, referred to the Middle Valley of the Rio Grande, occupied by Tiwa-speaking Indians, as the Province of Tiguex.

Francisco Vásquez de Coronado became the first European explorer to significantly affect the Province of Tiguex. The expedition was primarily looking for gold. The Coronado expedition was large, with about 350 soldiers; a large number of spouses, slaves and servants; and as many as two thousand Mexican Indian allies. The expedition also brought thousands of animals, including horses, mules, sheep and cattle.

The expedition entered present-day New Mexico from the west in 1540, and the military attachment attacked and conquered the Zuni Pueblo. Small forces from the expedition visited a number of pueblos in the Rio Grande and Pecos Valleys before selecting a place for the oncoming winter. The forward party of the expedition selected the Tiwa Pueblo of Coofor (one of many names, another of which is Puaray) as the site for the winter encampment. Coofor was about two miles south of Bernalillo on the west side of the Rio Grande.

Highway marker located just west of 1540 Coronado wintering site. *Roger Zimmerman Collection.*

Coronado needed to sustain his group, and in desperation, he ordered his men to simply take supplies that they needed. The expedition's livestock consumed much of the post-harvest cornstalks used by the Pueblos for cooking and heating during the winters, and this became a source of many conflicts. The Pueblos were facing survival problems, and these activities had a significant impact on them. There were skirmishes, and eventually the Tiwas vacated their villages during the winter of 1540. In 1541, Coronado set off in a foray across the Great Plains to central Kansas in his search for riches. The Tiwas returned to occupy their homes when the expedition left. The Tiwas abandoned them again upon the expedition's return in the fall and were happy to see Coronado and his expedition leave for good in 1542. Little did they know that his legacy was the addition of the horse to the Native American scene. Horses became invaluable assets as the Pueblos and other tribes hunted, gathered, traded and raided.

After the Coronado experience, the Spanish explorers used the Middle Valley of the Province of Tiguex as a passageway between Mexico and the northern pueblos along El Camino Real. Alameda, Isleta and Sandia Pueblos, on El Camino Real, apparently were vacated during periods of conflict.

A state official scenic historic marker for the Province of Tiguex is located near mile marker 10 on NM 528 in Rio Rancho. The marker is just west of what was thought to be the 1540 and 1541 wintering locations for the Coronado expedition. The highway marker discussing the Tiguex Province is one of many located throughout New Mexico.

Albuquerque has Tiguex Park, which is on the east side of Old Town on the intersection of Mountain Road and Nineteenth Street. A plaque is located in the park that discusses Tiguex Province history following the Pueblo Revolt in 1680.

## Tiwa Pueblos
Province of Tiguex

Three Province of Tiguex villages directly contributed to the initiation and eventual growth of Albuquerque. They are discussed in the context of being in existence before the Spanish came, being subjected to Spanish rule, participating in the Pueblo Revolt in 1680 and responding to the aftermath of the revolt. Also presented is information about the Coronado Historic Site, located at the ancient Tiwa pueblo of Kuaua.

## Isleta Pueblo
117 Tribal Road 40 #A
Isleta Pueblo, NM 87022
505-869-3111 | https://www.isletapueblo.com

Isleta Pueblo is a Native American village in the southern part of Bernalillo County that has existed since the 1300s. It is listed in the National Register of Historic Places. *Isleta* means "Little Island" in Spanish. Isleta is on the Rio

Highway marker identifying Isleta Pueblo.
*Roger Zimmerman Collection.*

Grande and was at an important crossroad for both Pueblo and Spanish trade routes. The Pueblo peoples developed agricultural practices and used primitive irrigation to grow such things as maize, beans, squash and cotton.

The village was located on El Camino Real and became an important stop for Spanish travelers. Isleta also became an important center of the advancement of Christianity in the 1600s. The Spanish mission San Agustin de la Isleta was built in 1629–30 and is the oldest major building in the Albuquerque area. It is reported that an earlier church had been built in 1612 or 1613.

Isleta took a passive role in the Pueblo Revolt of 1680 but became involved in subsequent activities in 1681. Departing Spaniards from the Santa Fe area, under the protection of Spanish governor Antonio de Otermin, took temporary refuge in the village when the revolt started. In November 1681, Governor Otermin returned to New Mexico with the goal of recapturing the province. He marched to Isleta Pueblo and fought a brief battle before accepting the village's surrender. The Puebloans feigned surrender while gathering a large force to oppose Otermin. Otermin was later militarily resisted at Sandia, Alameda and Puaray Pueblos.

On January 1, 1682, Otermin decided to return to El Paso, burning Isleta Pueblo and taking many people of Isleta with him as prisoners. Other surviving people from Isleta migrated to the Hopi villages in what was to become the state of Arizona for refuge. They didn't return until about 1710, when the pueblo was rebuilt.

Isleta Pueblo is just south of the NM 314/NM 147 intersection. A New Mexico Scenic Historical Highway Marker describing the pueblo is located at the intersection of NM 314 and nearby NM 45.

## Sandia Pueblo
481 Sandia Loop
Bernalillo, NM 87104
505-869-3317 | https://sandiapueblo.nsn.us

Sandia Pueblo is located north of Albuquerque and has an interesting history. Like Isleta Pueblo, it has been in existence as a village since the 1300s. It was reported to have a population of three thousand in the 1500s.

The Spanish mission San Francisco de Sandia was started in 1617. The church was partially burned by the revolting Indians in 1680, and the pueblo was burned by New Mexico governor Otermin when he passed by on the way to Texas in 1680. The residents hurriedly rebuilt the village, and then Otermin returned in 1681 in an attempt to regain the territory. He fought a battle at Isleta and then moved north through the Sandia Pueblo region. The people of the pueblo had fled to the Hopi villages in Arizona. Otermin burned what had been rebuilt, decided that he wasn't going to reconquer New Mexico and instead turned south and returned to El Paso.

The residents of Sandia Pueblo didn't return from the Hopi villages until 1742. It was reported that there were 350 residents in 1748. What is interesting is that the Spanish government protected the lands during this absence, and the people had a homeland to return to. The government was giving land titles to non-Indian lands, and somehow the pueblo was not overrun with Spanish land grants. There may have been another reason for this action. In 1762, the New Mexico governor ordered Sandia Pueblo to be rebuilt. He apparently wanted it as a buffer against Navajo and Apache raids. Whatever the reason, Sandia has remained as an active pueblo to this day.

The New Mexico Scenic Historical Highway Marker Sandia Pueblo is on NM 313 about 3.5 miles north of the NM 313/NM 422 roundabout.

Highway marker identifying Sandia Pueblo. *Roger Zimmerman Collection.*

## Alameda Village/Neighborhood
Intersection Alameda Boulevard/Fourth Street
Albuquerque, NM

Alameda was a village in the Province of Tiguex before Coronado came in 1540. The Pueblo was situated primarily on the east bank of the Rio Grande about seven miles north of downtown Albuquerque. It was burned during the Pueblo Revolt. Efforts to revive the village in the early 1700s were not successful, and the pueblo was abandoned.

After the Tiwa Indian people abandoned Alameda Pueblo, a land grant covering the pueblo townsite was given to a Spanish citizen by the governor of New Mexico in 1710. This is an example of how the Spanish government handled non-Indian lands. The land grant, covering some eighty-nine thousand acres, was given in the name of King Philip IV of Spain to Francisco Montes Vigil. Vigil later sold the land to Captain Juan Gonzáles of the Spanish army. The land has gone through many ownerships and court battles since that time.

Alameda Boulevard is a major street in the Alameda neighborhood. The boulevard leads to the Alameda Bridge over the Rio Grande, which enters Corrales immediately to the west of the bridge. The village of Corrales got its name due to the extensive corrals that the original land grant owner, Francisco Montes Vigil, built and used on the west side of the river.

Alameda has a New Mexico Scenic Historical Highway Marker. It is located on NM 313 just south of the NM 313/NM 422 roundabout. It is just south of the bridge over the North Diversion Ditch.

Side one (left) and side two (right) highway marker identifying Alameda Pueblo. *Roger Zimmerman Collection.*

## Coronado Historic Site

485 Kuaua Street
Bernalillo, NM 87004
505-867-5351 | http://nmhistoricsites.org/coronado

Another Tiwa village is listed here not for its relevance to Albuquerque history, but to help provide information about the early Province of Tiguex and also documentation about the Coronado expedition. The Coronado Historic Site is at the Kuaua Pueblo, which was one of the pueblos involved in the Tiguex War with Coronado. Kuaua was the northernmost village in the original Province of Tiguex.

The visitors' center is divided into two parts: Coronado and Native American. The Coronado exhibit is small but helpful. The Kuaua Pueblo site has ruins from more than 1,200 rooms. It is highlighted with a square kiva that was used by the natives, and the murals in the kiva show fine examples of pre-Columbian art.

The historic site is across the Rio Grande just west of Bernalillo, New Mexico, and north of US 550. The site is close to Santa Ana Pueblo, which is a Keresan-speaking pueblo north of Bernalillo, New Mexico.

Part of Coronado display at Coronado Historic Site near Bernalillo, New Mexico. *Roger Zimmerman Collection.*

# SPANISH PROVINCE OF SANTA FE DE NUEVO MÉXICO

The next significant invasion of the Province of Tiguex occurred in 1598, but occupation of the pueblos was not a goal of the expedition. Juan de Oñate y Salazar was a conquistador from New Spain, and his task was to establish the Province of Santa Fe de Nuevo México. He was to select a headquarters site and be the first colonial governor of the province. The Oñate party is reported to have consisted of 130 families, 270 single men, several Franciscan priests and about seven thousand head of livestock.

Oñate and his party traveled through the Province of Tiguex and eventually settled at San Gabriel, which was close to the Tewa-speaking pueblo of San Juan de los Caballeros north of Santa Fe. This pueblo is more recently known as Ohkay Owingeh. Oñate thought that the northern pueblos would be more hospitable when he chose San Gabriel as the location for his headquarters.

In October 1598, a squad of Oñate's Spanish soldiers demanded supplies from Acoma Pueblo, and a conflict ensued. The pueblo inhabitants felt that the food was needed for their survival. They resisted, and several Spaniards were killed. In January 1599, Oñate retaliated by destroying the pueblo and massacring many Acoma residents and maiming others. Oñate continued exploring in 1601 in the plains at a location that was to become the modern state of Oklahoma. He scheduled other excursions, culminating with a Colorado River expedition in 1604. Oñate was recalled to Mexico City in 1606 for a hearing regarding his conduct. He was tried and convicted of cruelty to both natives and colonists.

Map showing province of Santa Fe de Nuevo México, 1820. *Paul Zimmerman compilation.*

Oñate's successor was Don Pedro de Peralta. Peralta came in 1609 and almost immediately moved the capital of the province from San Gabriel to Santa Fe, primarily because the latter was at the end of El Camino Real and this location was the center of trade. Santa Fe was started as a group of homes formed as a Tanoan village. Tewa-speaking natives had settled along the Santa Fe River, which had year-round flow. The cluster of native homes is near the site of today's plaza. The site had a trading post and soon became a center for trade on El Camino Real.

The Spanish Crown, through Governor Peralta, began demonstrating an active interest in promoting a missionary program in an effort to civilize and assimilate the Pueblo Indians into the province. With considerable support from the Spanish government, the Catholic Church launched a massive drive to convert the native people to Christianity and erect majestic missions in key locations. Within the Province of Tiguex, Sandia and Isleta Pueblos were to have full-scale churches with accompanying priest quarters, workrooms and classrooms. The churches even had organs to add to the quality of the services. Lesser missions were built at Puaray (now extinct) and Alameda (extinct as a pueblo).

The church directed the priests to stamp out the native religions. Pagan Indian religion was seen as coming from the devil. Masks and fetishes were burned, and native priests were considered sorcerers. They outlawed Kachina-type dances. There was only one way to worship God, they felt, and the priests exhibited an inflexibility in accepting anything short of total transformation to a Spanish-style Christianity.

Another issue developed when the settlers and officials exploited the native people. Spanish law prohibited colonists from interfering with native customs or the taking of native property. This law was ignored by the settlers, as Spain could not enforce it. Native men were pulled off their fields during harvest season to administer to the needs of the colonists. In some cases, natives became forced laborers or were made slaves of the occupying Spanish.

Other factors emerged. A severe drought came in the 1670s and threatened food supplies for all residents, indigenous and immigrant. Also, a significant health problem arose when the pueblos began declining in population because of diseases brought from the Old World. Native populations had no established immunity to measles, smallpox and other such afflictions, and the results caused measurable population declines. In the latter part of the 1600s, the population in the Province of Tiguex had diminished significantly, and survivors had moved to the larger villages of Sandia, Isleta, Alameda and Puaray.

The Native Americans in the Province of Santa Fe de Nuevo México became fed up with the Spanish during the seventeenth century. The Pueblo Revolt was an uprising of the indigenous Pueblo people against the Spanish colonizers. The revolt started on August 10, 1680, in Taos Pueblo. The organizer, Po'pay, enlisted primarily northern pueblos in an uprising that ended up in Santa Fe. The goal was that inhabitants from each Pueblo would rise up and kill the Spanish in their area, and then all would advance on Santa Fe to kill or expel all the remaining Spanish from the entire province of Santa Fe de Nuevo México. On August 10, Puebloans stole Spanish horses to prevent them from fleeing, sealed off roads leading to Santa Fe and pillaged Spanish settlements. A total of four hundred people were killed, and twenty-one of thirty-three Franciscan missionaries were also killed.

Initially, people in Isleta took a passive role in the Pueblo Revolt. Spanish survivors fled to Santa Fe and then to Isleta Pueblo. Tiwa-speaking Pueblos at Sandia, Puaray and Alameda did participate. At Sandia, the church was looted, vandalized and burned by the retreating Indians, and Governor

Otermin, in retribution, burned the pueblo during his retreat. Puaray and Alameda Pueblos were burned, and the missions were looted and vandalized as well.

The Spanish reconquest of the New Mexico province was organized by Diego de Vargas, who marched to Santa Fe unopposed in August 1692. He promised clemency and protection to the one thousand Pueblo people assembled if they would swear allegiance to the king of Spain and return to the Christian faith. Initially, the Pueblos rejected the offer, but they finally accepted it on September 14, 1692. Vargas went back to Mexico in 1692 and returned in 1693 with eight hundred people, including one hundred soldiers. This time, seventy Pueblo warriors and four hundred family members within Santa Fe opposed his entry. Governor Vargas and his forces staged a quick and bloody recapture of the town, with the imprisonment and later execution of the seventy warriors. Other skirmishes followed, with eventual complete reconquest occurring by 1700.

The Pueblo Revolt gained the Pueblo Indians three important concessions from the Spanish. First, there was a measure of freedom from future Spanish efforts to eradicate their culture and religion following the reconquest. The Franciscan priests returning to New Mexico did not attempt to impose another theocracy. Pueblos were allowed to practice their traditional religions alongside practicing Catholicism. This was a very important concession by the church hierarchy, and it has worked since. The Catholic Church still has a prominent presence in Native American pueblos more than three hundred years later. As an example, in 2007, I went to the Catholic church at Acoma Pueblo and witnessed a traditional Pueblo dance with Kachina-like dancers.

Another concession was that the Spanish would not force the Pueblo Indians into becoming slaves. The Spanish did not have any right to force a Native American person into servitude. This promise was taken seriously and went hand in hand with the improvements in church relations with the Native Americans.

The third concession was that the Spanish would respect Indian lands so that Pueblos would have lands that would be protected by the Spanish government. The Spanish even set up special tribunals to handle Indian land claims. The discussions of the awarding of a Spanish land grant to families living in the Alameda region is a testament to the fact that if the land were abandoned, it was up for grabs by the Spanish government, yet the lands around Sandia Pueblo were protected during their temporary resettlement at the Hopi Pueblo.

## Plaza for Villa de Alburquerque
303 Romero Street NW
Albuquerque, NM 87104
505-221-6490

During his return to New Mexico in 1693, Diego de Vargas needed to solidify the Spanish occupation of the region. He founded villages and places of limited government operations, short of being called the more formal government organization "villa," like Bernalillo and Atrisco, in an effort to spread Spanish influence to the rural areas. On April 8, 1704, Governor Vargas died suddenly while on a mission to restore order to the province. His successor started Albuquerque.

Don Francisco Cuervo y Valdéz was appointed governor of the Province of Santa Fe de Nuevo México by the viceroy of New Spain, the Duke of Alburquerque, who was the head of Spanish activities in north America. Cuervo had been a loyal public servant in Mexico before this promotion. Cuervo arrived in Santa Fe on March 10, 1705, and slightly over a year later, by July 30, 1706, the job had been given to someone else by the king. Within this short period of time, the Villa de Alburquerque was started.

One of the responsibilities of a province governor was to establish Spanish villas. A villa in this context was a fully chartered town with specific rights and privileges extended by the Crown. A villa was to have three things: (1) protection for the inhabitants; (2) a church; and (3) an established community that was built around a plaza containing government structures. Santa Cruz was the villa for the Upper Valley and Santa Fe the villa for the capital. Governor Vargas was setting up Bernalillo to be the villa for the Middle Valley of the Rio Grande. Bernalillo had a plaza laid out, and a church had been built. After Governor Vargas's death, his successor, Governor Cuervo de Valdéz, decided to change things and selected the land in the lower Middle Valley as the location of the next villa.

Governor Cuervo selected some high ground near the Rio Grande as the site. The land had been occupied since 1632 and, in 1706, was the site of a hacienda belonging to Doña Luisa de Trujillo, who was the widow of Francisco de Trujillo. Governor Cuervo stated in his petition to the king on April 23, 1706, "I certify to the King, our Lord, and to the most excellent senior viceroy: That I founded a villa on the banks and in the valley of the Rio del Norte in a good place as regards land, water, pasture, and firewood. I gave it as patron saint the glorious apostle of the Indies, San Francisco Xavier, and called and named it villa de Alburquerque." The Rio del Norte was an early name for the upper part of the Rio Grande.

It is beyond the scope of this book to try to explain the happenings related to the certification that was made by Governor Cuervo and the actions that followed. Basically, the governor said in documentation supporting the certification that among the accomplishments were: (1) thirty-five families had taken up residence; (2) a spacious church had been completed; (3) a house for a priest was underway; and (4) there was a start for government buildings for the local officials.

For years, irregularities about the founding of Alburquerque festered in Madrid. Finally, in 1712, the Crown issued a royal *cédula*, or decree, directing the current governor of the province to open an inquiry investigating whether Alburquerque had been legally founded or not. The investigation showed the discrepancies in the founding. Deviations from the truth included that there were fewer than twenty charter families and that there was no church, house for the priest or government buildings. There wasn't even an established plaza.

Governor Cuervo had cleverly named the villa after the viceroy of New Spain, the Duke of Alburquerque, and that probably was a major factor in the Spanish government resisting the temptation to decertify the villa. The

Old Town scenic marker describing major historic features. *Roger Zimmerman Collection.*

Gazebo on Old Town Plaza. *Roger Zimmerman Collection.*

investigation came to the conclusion that Governor Cuervo had stretched the truth, but in the end, it was decided that inasmuch as the town was already up and growing, the members judged that for the general welfare of the realm, it could be permitted to continue.

Even though the starting of Albuquerque was a sham, the thinking behind the certification was not faulty. Governor Cuervo saw that the land was spacious and had good water. The area had been in a drought since the 1670s, and the Middle Valley offered continuity in water supplies for farming. Second, the townsite was a few feet higher than the Rio Grande and offered some protection for periodic flooding. Third, trees were readily available for firewood. Fourth, it lay astride El Camino Real, and good fords across the Rio Grande existed to the south and west. Finally, the Middle Valley was located at the mouth of Tijeras Arroyo and served as a good place to resist the marauding Apaches, and it was not in the middle of a number of Tiguex villages that were recovering from the trauma of the Pueblo Revolt. He felt the villa could survive and defend itself. Most likely he saw better potential for future growth in

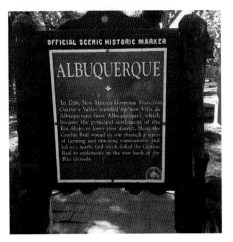

Historic marker on Old Town Plaza (the reason for the misspelling of Albuquerque is not clear). *Roger Zimmerman Collection.*

Albuquerque than at Bernalillo, and in this respect, he was correct. Governor Cuervo probably never knew the wisdom of his decision.

The founding of Alburquerque created an issue. The villa was created in honor of the Duke of Alburquerque, and this name lasted for some time. Gradually, residents in New Spain dropped the first *r*, and the community became known as Albuquerque.

Throughout history, this plaza was the location for many historical events. Spanish culture promotes town life with religious observances, public markets and social activity within a political structure. A plaza was that prominent place that was at the center of activities. This book will describe many of them. A 121-foot flagpole was erected in the center of the plaza by the U.S. Army in the 1850s. A gazebo now stands there.

A visitors' center for Old Town exists on Romero Street. It is located on the west side of the plaza. Useful walking tour and visitor information can be found at the center.

## San Felipe de Neri Church
2005 North Plaza NW
Albuquerque, NM 87104
505-243-4628

The San Francisco Xavier Church was established in 1706 under Fray Manuel Moreno, a Franciscan missionary. The exact location of the church is uncertain, but it was thought to be on the west side of the plaza. In July 1706, there was a royal decree that had just been received in Mexico City indicating that the next villa established was to be called San Felipe de Neri in honor of King Philip V. Governor Cuervo had already established a villa in honor of San Francisco Xavier the previous April. The governor cleverly responded to the king's action by changing

*Above*: San Felipe de Neri Church, established in 1793, circa 1945. *Albuquerque Museum, 1982.180.851, Barnes and Caplin Gift.*

*Left*: Salvador Armijo House, built circa 1840. *Roger Zimmerman Collection.*

the town's name to San Felipe de Alburquerque, thus jointly honoring the king and viceroy.

The church people were not as prompt. The first church was started in 1706 and completed by 1719. Construction details are not available. The cemetery was located east of the church, and the convent (rectory) was to the south. Fray Francisco Dominquez visited the church in 1776 and noted that the painting of the patron saint in the church was still San Francisco Xavier and not San Felipe Neri. A correction needed to be made. Not much happened, and the existing church was allowed to deteriorate in the late 1700s to the point where it collapsed during the winter of 1792.

The San Felipe de Neri Church was begun in 1793 and is still a functioning parish church. The new church was cruciform in shape and had twin bell towers. The walls are five feet thick. The church was located on the north side of the plaza. The church has been remodeled several times. Except for its tin ceiling, brick floor and south entrance, today's church is the same structure as in 1793.

Five properties in Old Town are listed in the National Register of Historic Places. The San Felipe de Neri Church is one. The others are:

- Charles A. Bottger House (1912), 110 San Felipe NW
- Our Lady of the Angels School (1878), 320 Romero Street NW
- Antonio Vigil House (1879), 413 Romero Street NW
- Salvador Armijo House (1840), 618 Rio Grande Boulevard NW

## La Placita Restaurant
208 San Felipe Street NW
Albuquerque, NM 87104
505-247-2204

One of the contributions that the Spanish conquest made to the New World was the addition of Spanish Colonial architecture. Missions provided the best evidence of the influence of the Spanish on architecture. Friars were responsible for construction of the missions, and the Pueblo people provided the labor. Glass, nails and hardware were generally not available. Local materials had to be used. Flat roofs were popular, with *vigas* and *latillas* furnishing the ceiling support. Thick adobe walls were

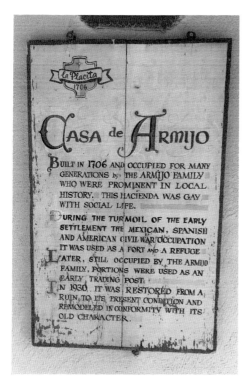

Sign outside La Placita Restaurant indicating the history of the building. *Roger Zimmerman Collection.*

constructed, and mud plaster was applied. The floors were earthen. Wooden bars were used on windows.

Spanish architecture was used for homes, churches, businesses and government buildings. The photo here of the sign on one of the older buildings, the La Placita Restaurant, explains that the buildings did not always remain as originally constructed.

The restaurant is on the site of the Ambrosio Armijo family homestead. Ambrosio built his home and store next to the family headquarters on San Felipe Street on the southeast corner of the plaza in the 1880s. The property at this location was used to house the County Seat from 1854 to 1878 and for classrooms before the public schools were established. Long a county commissioner, Ambrosio had two sons, Mariano and Perfecto, who had prominent roles in developing Albuquerque after the railroad came. Ambrosio's brother, Manuel, was a three-time governor of the Mexican Territory and was the person who yielded the territory to General Kearny in 1846.

One of the weaknesses of the adobe-style Spanish architecture was the vulnerability to flooding. A severe flood in 1874 covered the floodplain of the Middle Valley, where what was to become New Town was under water. Old Town was an island in the floodplain, but the island was threatened. Shopkeepers in Old Town loaded what merchandise they could salvage into wagons and fled, while the majority of residents escaped to the hills on the east, where they lived for days in tents. Residential-style adobe buildings suffered in the flood, and this may be a partial explanation of why the La Placita building needed to be restored in 1930.

## Atrisco Land Grant Community

2708 Rosendo Garcia SW
Atrisco, NM 87105
505-433-1905

After the Pueblo Revolt, the Spanish issued substantial land grants to each pueblo and appointed a public defender to protect the rights of the Indians and argue their legal cases in Spanish courts. There were to be Indian lands and open lands outside the Indian lands that Spain would control. The land grants were partially justified by the declines in populations and migrations of the pueblo inhabitants to a few villages. For instance, the remaining villages in the Province of Tiguex after the Pueblo Revolt of 1680 were Sandia, Isleta and Alameda. Alameda was disbanded by 1710.

The Spanish government issued land grants to Spanish settlers in the lands not assigned to the Pueblos. The settlers could settle the land, have personal title to the land around their haciendas and have grazing rights on specific tracts of adjoining land. The title to the grazing land remained with the Crown. Mexico separated from Spain, and the U.S. government took over the region in later years. Land grant issues originating from some of the Spanish practices are still being contested in New Mexico and federal courts.

Early Spanish settlers found good farm and grazing lands in the region in the twenty-seven miles between Isleta and Sandia Pueblos, particularly below the village of Alameda, and started occupying them in the early 1600s. The family of Don Pedro y Chaves had settled in the Atrisco area in the mid-1600s. It became unoccupied during the Pueblo Revolt of 1680–92.

Governor Vargas established many land grants in the Albuquerque region after the revolt. One went to Fernando Duran y Chaves, son of

Don Pedro y Chaves, in 1692. The land grant of Atrisco was given on the condition that he personally settle it and develop it with other settlers. This was land that his father had occupied before the revolt. Duran y Chaves did what was required and gained formal possession in 1703. Initially, some forty-one thousand acres were involved. The land grant was extended by nearly twenty-six thousand acres in 1768 to accommodate the increasing Atrisco population.

Atrisco is an unincorporated community in Bernalillo County. The community is bounded to the east, west and north by the city of Albuquerque. It is the region between Bridge Street and Central Avenue west of the Rio Grande. Atrisco Boulevard runs north–south through the community.

## Barelas Neighborhood
801 Barelas Road SW
Albuquerque, NM 87102
505-848-1343

The settlement was originally established in 1662 and is known as the oldest neighborhood in the city. Barelas was the site of an important river crossing of El Camino Real on the Rio Grande. The community consists of a triangular area bounded by Coal Avenue on the north, the railroad tracks on the east and the Rio Grande on the west.

The Acequia Madre de Barelas was constructed around 1830 to irrigate fields on the east side of the Middle Valley. The *acequia* started above Alameda and went down the east side of the valley, through what was to become Martineztown and on to Barelas, where it returned to the Rio Grande. The grade of the *acequia* was set so that irrigation water would be available for the farmers and other land users.

There was a pond near Martineztown that served as a moderator for floodwaters coming from the foothills to the east. A drain to the pond was the Lower Barelas Canal, which went west, crossed El Camino Real and passed under what was to become the railroad tracks before turning south and crossing Railroad (Central) Avenue between Second and Third Streets.

The Barelas neighborhood blossomed when the railroad came, transforming from a quiet farming village to a busy blue-collar neighborhood. Most of Barelas was incorporated into what became

New Albuquerque in 1891. The Barelas neighborhood saw increased prosperity after Fourth Street, one of the main north–south arteries through the neighborhood, was designated as part of Route 66 in 1926. The road was soon lined with filling stations, garages and cafés catering to the steady stream of travelers passing through.

# CHANGING GOVERNMENTS
# AND EXPANDED TRADE

S pain was the first of four governments that had jurisdiction over the Albuquerque region. Spain started the Province of Santa Fe de Nuevo México in 1598, and this continued until 1821, when Mexico separated from Spain. Mexico called the Spanish province the Territory of Santa Fe de Nuevo México.

Two major changes in governments led to the eventual placement of the Territory of Santa Fe de Nuevo México in the Republic of Mexico. This all occurred during the period of 1808–23. The first change occurred in Spain, and the second related to Mexican independence.

The major changes in Spain occurred over a twelve-year period. Ferdinand VII became the absolute monarch in 1808 and then was put into exile by Napoleon later that year. He remained in exile while Napoleon's brother, Joseph Bonaparte I, served as the emperor of Spain until December 1813. During the reign of Joseph Bonaparte, Spanish citizens organized an interim Spanish government, the Supreme Central Junta, and called for a *cortes* (congress) to convene with representatives from all of the off-shore provinces in an effort to establish a firm claim to legitimacy. A *cortes* was called in 1810, and the Constitution of 1812, sometimes called the "Cortes of Cádiz," was eventually passed. The *cortes* had representatives from the remote provinces as well as the peninsula in Europe. New Mexico had a representative attend this constitutional convention in Spain as one of seven from New Spain. The principal aim of the new constitution was the prevention of arbitrary and corrupt royal rule. It provided for a limited monarchy that was governed by ministers subject to parliamentary control rather than absolute control from a monarch. There was no special provision in the new constitution-based government for the church or the nobility to be involved in governance, and this was a major change in philosophy and a threat to those functions.

Ferdinand VII came back into power in 1814 with the agreement that he would serve as a constitutional emperor rather than an absolute emperor. Nuevo México was quite a distance from Mexico City and an ocean away from Spain; however, the events in Spain had an influence on it. The new constitutional monarchy in 1814 called for the creation of local governments, called *ayuntamientos*, which would provide representative governments at the local level. All towns with populations greater than one thousand within the Spanish realm were to elect local governments. Albuquerque, Bernalillo and Belen had *ayuntamientos* in 1814–15. *Ayuntamientos* were formed by popular election according to the 1812 constitution. In an *ayuntamiento*, a municipal council had magistrates, councilors and a secretary. By contrast, under an absolute monarch, communities had *alcaldes* (mayors).

Ferdinand VII reneged on this promise to lead a constitutional monarchy soon after he took office. He restored his absolute monarchy in 1814. However, it took some time for the communications to Nuevo México to reflect this; finally, in 1815, the *ayuntamiento* was disbanded and an *alcalde* reinstated. Public unrest continued through the rest of the decade in Spain, and Ferdinand VII's government was later overthrown by rebels in 1820, when he agreed to be a constitutional emperor again. This status lasted for several years. During this change in government structure in Spain, Mexico separated in 1821, and this action terminated the influence of Spain in New Spain.

The residents of New Spain were suffering somewhat from the excesses of the Spanish monarchy and were starting to think about separation from Spain as early as 1810. Rebellious actions started that year with the "Cry of Dolores." Dissatisfaction continued through the next decade, and when Ferdinand VII had to change to become a constitutional monarch in 1820, the residents in New Spain were looking for a new direction; Mexico formally withdrew from Spain in 1821. The leaders of the rebellion from Spain emphasized three guarantees: Mexico was to be a Catholic empire, independent from Spain and united against its enemies.

The intention at separation was that Mexico would be a monarchy with a strong Catholic Church influence, unlike the government that was evolving in Spain under the Constitution of 1812. The Mexican Congress in 1822 created the First Mexican Empire, with army leader Agustín de Iturbide as the emperor. The First Mexican Empire soon came to an end, and the First Mexican Republic followed. A republic was proclaimed on November 1, 1823, and governing power was managed by a constituent Congress. Mexico continued to rule with some form of constitution-based government until the Americans came in 1846. The Catholic Church had a prominent role in governmental activities.

Citizens of Nuevo México adjusted to the changes, but the First Mexican Empire and later Mexican Republic encouraged trade with the United States, while Spain had prohibited it. This change in trade policy led to the establishment of the Santa Fe Trail in 1821.

With the benefit of the establishment of the Santa Fe Trail, citizens of Albuquerque thrived with the new trade-based economy. Albuquerque was a way station that benefited from the increased flow of traffic up and down El Camino Real. Landowners were becoming prosperous in ranching and sheep raising. Families with names like Chavez, Armijo, Perea, Otero and Baca became involved in mercantile enterprises and did well. These families formed an upper crust of settlers that dominated political, economic and social life between Bernalillo and Belen. There was considerable intermarrying between the families. The dominant family in the Albuquerque region was Armijo.

Independence from Spain led to a new prosperity in Albuquerque. The emergence of the Santa Fe Trail provided trade opportunities that were not available with El Camino Real, and there was an expansion of wealth. Landowners could get some of the frills and luxuries that were hard to get while Spain ruled. People from the Middle Valley hitched up their wagons and journeyed east to buy trade wares that changed nice homes into elegant haciendas with tasteful furnishings. Merchants set up stores around the plaza and prospered with the influx of trading goods and the demand for them.

Albuquerque became a convenient anchor for the traders on the Santa Fe Trail. It was more than two thousand feet lower in elevation and had a longer growing season. With the convenience of Rio Grande water, farming, ranching and sheepherding activities flourished. The plaza became a major trading center where traders could bring products in the Middle Valley and return with produce and wool-based products. Enterprising businessmen and professionals migrated to Albuquerque.

Migration to Albuquerque was not easy. The Santa Fe trail was a challenging nine hundred miles from Independence, Missouri, to Santa Fe, New Mexico. Users of the trail faced hot and dry summers and long and cold winters. Fresh water was scarce. There was always the threat attacks by Comanches and Apaches. The Native Americans felt that the high plains were theirs and resisted any intrusions by the trespassers on the trail. The Comanches were a special threat because they stole horses and mules whenever possible. In fact, the trail organizers enlarged the sizes of the convoys to deter attacks and changed to using slow-moving oxen, which weren't sought by the Comanches.

# EL CAMINO REAL

El Camino Real entered the Albuquerque region of the Middle Valley just south of Barelas. Much of the area south of what is now Central Avenue and the community of Barelas was situated in open pastureland without trees and was composed of swamps and shallow ponds. The swamp near Barelas was known as the Esteros de Mejía (Swamp of Mejía). The land was unfit for farming.

One of the features for travel along El Camino Real was the establishment of *parajes*, spots where travelers customarily stopped for the night. *Parajes* were spaced to accommodate a daily ride by a convoy. The Hacienda de Mejía was a *paraje* that was established on El Camino Real in the Barelas region. The hacienda was just north of a crossing of the Rio Grande and was most likely a welcome stopping point after traversing the river.

El Camino Real reached a fork in the vicinity of the swamps near Barelas. One branch went to what was to become Old Town Albuquerque and traveled along what was to become Eighth through Twelfth Streets. The other branch went essentially north from the hacienda and took the higher ground near the sand hills in a direct route toward Alameda. The railroad was later located just west of this branch.

## Plaza de la Constitución
303 Romero Street NW
Albuquerque, NM 87104
505-221-6490

When Ferdinand VII was restored to power in March 1814, he had promised to uphold the new constitution. There were many effects from this arrangement throughout the Spanish kingdom. In 1814, the Villa de Alburquerque had held an election, and an *ayuntamiento* was created, much to the pleasure of the inhabitants. Within a matter of weeks after being reinstated as the constitutional monarch, encouraged by conservatives and the nobility and backed by the Roman Catholic Church hierarchy, Ferdinand abolished the Constitution of 1812 and restored the absolute monarchy. Response in Nuevo México was slow, and it wasn't until 1815 that the *ayuntamiento* was dissolved and an *alcalde* reinstalled. Actions like this probably helped citizens of Spain and New Spain push for the restoring of a constitutional monarchy.

Albuquerque citizens apparently were enthused about the effects of the Constitution of 1812. The constitution officially made the colonies of Spain part of the empire and thus entitled to representation in the Spanish *Cortes*. In the 1820–21 period, Albuquerque's plaza was renamed the *Plaza de la Constitución* in honor of the Constitution of 1812. The recognition apparently signaled the desire of the people to formally recognize the constitutional type of government that they had experienced with the *ayuntamiento* during the 1814–15 period.

It is interesting that the renaming of the plaza occurred during the end of the Spanish rule and survived the beginning and 1823 ending of the First Mexican Empire.

# INCLUDED COMMUNITIES AND NEIGHBORHOODS

Albuquerque is surrounded by communities and neighborhoods that have distinct histories. Many were formed around farms or ranches by families. Each has a unique and interesting history. It is beyond the scope of this book to try to include this information, but some—like Alameda, Atrisco and Barelas—have already been introduced and discussed. Four others are identified and described here to serve as location references for other discussions.

## Martineztown Neighborhood
8085 Edith Boulevard NE
Albuquerque, NM 87102
505-242-4333

Martineztown is a small neighborhood in Albuquerque that is immediately northeast of downtown and east of the railroad tracks. It started as a small farming village in the 1850s and has retained much of its original charm. The neighborhood has winding streets, irregular lots and adobe buildings typical of older Hispanic communities in northern New Mexico. Irrigation for farming was provided by the Acequia Madre del los Barelas, which had its source near Alameda and brought water to the downstream community of Barelas. Martineztown was annexed by New Albuquerque in 1898.

Martineztown is east of Broadway Boulevard between Martin Luther King Avenue and Lomas Boulevard. It extends as far east as High Street.

## Los Griegos Neighborhood
1231 Candelaria Road NW
Albuquerque, NM 87107
505-761-4050

The neighborhood of Los Griegos is located in the North Valley area generally between Fourth Street and the Rio Grande and between Candelaria and Montaño Avenues. Los Griegos was originally a grant of lands given to Juan Griego in 1708 and annexed by Albuquerque in the late 1940s and early 1950s. It is in the National Register of Historic Places.

The Los Griegos Historic District is locally significant because it is the only nineteenth-century village in Albuquerque's North Valley that has retained its architectural continuity and cultural traditions. The buildings in Los Griegos are the embodiment of a unique culture that has its base in eighteenth-century Spanish customs. Most buildings in the district are single-story, stuccoed and built of *terrónes*, which are sod blocks cut from marshlands near the river. The vernacular style continues into the twentieth century in Los Griegos, with the buildings maintaining a modest appearance.

A major *acequia* that fed Old Town was called the Acequia Madre de Los Griegos. It had its source near the community and ran down a channel east of Old Town and then returned to the Rio Grande.

## Village of Corrales

4324 Corrales Road
Corrales, NM 87048
505-897-0502

Corrales is a village in Sandoval County, just north and west of Alameda. With proximity to the Rio Grande, the village was founded for agricultural purposes. It was incorporated as Corrales in 1971 to provide for increased service and control over development. As the population near the city of Albuquerque exploded after World War II, the charm and quiet ambiance of Corrales attracted many newcomers. Vast farming lands, beautiful vistas and the small-community feel continue to attract visitors. Today, the village is a rural residential community nestled between metropolitan Albuquerque and the burgeoning city of Rio Rancho.

The village contains the historic Casa San Ysidro, a restored Spanish hacienda from the 1700s, and Old San Ysidro Church, which was built in the 1860s and added to the National Register of Historic Places in 1980. It is also listed in the New Mexico Register of Cultural Properties.

Today, the Old San Ysidro Church is maintained, preserved and managed by volunteers of Corrales Historical Society using the monies earned from membership dues, fundraising events, donations and leasing income. The Corrales Historical Society (CHS) invites visitors to take a tour of the beautiful old church.

## Village of Los Ranchos de Albuquerque

6718 Rio Grande Boulevard
Los Ranchos, NM 87107
505-344-6582

The village of Los Ranchos is an incorporated municipality bordering Albuquerque, which was formed under the laws of the State of New Mexico on December 29, 1958. The original Los Ranchos townsite was located between Guadalupe Trail and Rio Grande, north of Chavez and south of Los Ranchos. The population of Los Ranchos was about five thousand in the 2000 census.

The area containing the village of Los Ranchos has been settled by humans for at least 2,500 years. During the Spanish Colonial period, there was a series of adobe villages scattered throughout the North Valley, including a community settled around a small plaza called San Jose de Los Ranchos. When New Mexico became a U.S. territory in 1850, this community was the Bernalillo County seat from 1850 to 1854.

Los Ranchos and the North Valley historically were agricultural settlements. By 1920, however, much of the land was out of production because of recurrent flooding and poor drainage. Some of the fields had developed high alkaline contents because of drainage limitations. This led to the formation of the Middle Rio Grande Conservancy District in the 1920s to implement drainage and flood-control improvements in the extended Middle Valley. A vast system of levees, ditches, laterals, drains and canals was created.

Besides improving the situation for agriculture, this development opened the area to increased land development. When World War II and its aftermath brought a population explosion to the Albuquerque region, the Los Ranchos area became ripe for development associated with the boom. The local residents did not want to be associated with the development of land in their region, which would be used to support population growth and the land-use demands of subdivisions. Concern over this type of growth helped lead to the incorporation of the modern village in the late 1950s.

# AMERICAN CITIZENSHIP

**A**lbuquerque was in the Territory of Santa Fe de Nuevo México until 1846, when Stephen W. Kearny arrived and claimed the territory for the United States. This change, coming at the start of the Mexican-American War, led in 1850 to the establishment of the U.S. territory of New Mexico.

The Mexican-American War was an armed conflict between the United States and Mexico during the period 1846–48. It followed in the wake of the 1845 U.S. annexation of the independent Republic of Texas as the twenty-eighth state of the Union. Mexico had not recognized the independence of the Republic of Texas and still considered it as a wayward territory whose boundaries were in question, and this uncertainty was in effect when the republic became a state. There is an interesting history about why and how Texas became independent, but suffice it to say, the republic did separate from Mexico and eventually became a state in the United States.

One of the major issues that arose when the Republic of Texas was formed was the establishment of boundaries. Texas claimed that its southern boundary was defined by the Rio Grande, and Mexico claimed that the southern boundary was the Nueces River; this issue was never settled. On the western boundary, Texas claimed the territory between the Rio Grande and the Arkansas River. These boundaries meant that land in Santa Fe de Nuevo México east of the Rio Grande belonged to the republic. This was an extensive body of land that had not been occupied by the Texans. Mexico generally agreed that the Rio Grande was the western boundary up to about El Paso, where the Territory of Santa Fe de Nuevo México came into play. Mexico did not relinquish its claim on this long-held Spanish/Mexican territory and, in doing so, retained the right to try to reclaim the contested land.

The United States accepted Texas as a state with the provision that the boundary issue with Mexico would have to be settled. The United States was going through a presidential election in 1844, and one of the issues was Manifest Destiny. Some in the country thought that it was their destiny to occupy the land west of the Mississippi River all the way to the Pacific Ocean. There was serious opposition to this, but in the end, President James Polk, who campaigned on Manifest Destiny, won the election and was sworn in as president on March 4, 1845. By December of that year, Texas had become a state, and in January 1846, President Polk challenged the southern boundary issue with Mexico. The United States sent a small contingent of troops south of the Nueces River to the banks of the Rio Grande. Mexican troops came across the Rio Grande and attacked the U.S. forces. Twelve soldiers were killed and fifty-two others captured. These same Mexican soldiers laid siege to a new American fort established along the Rio Grande. President Polk cited this as an invasion of U.S. territory and requested that Congress declare war. War was declared on Mexico on March 13, 1846.

In June 1846, General Stephen W. Kearny started a march westward toward the Mexican frontier with about 1,700 United States troops. His goal was to occupy the Mexican territories of Santa Fe de Nuevo México and Alta California (Upper California). His force left Bent's Fort on the Arkansas River in what is now southeastern Colorado and entered the contested territory claimed by both Texas and Mexico.

On August 15, 1846, General Kearny reached Las Vegas, New Mexico. General Kearny proclaimed New Mexico to be part of U.S. territory in a speech on the plaza. General Kearny then marched toward Santa Fe, expecting to be resisted by Mexican-supported forces. On August 18, 1846, Governor Manuel Armijo, appointed by the government of Mexico, left the scene of the anticipated battle at Apache Creek, south and east of Santa Fe, without a fight. General Kearny then entered Santa Fe, where he established a territorial government that was primarily led by the military until 1850. During this process, New Mexicans were declared to be citizens of the United States.

Following the military activities, there were two major actions by the U.S. government that affected the status of the Albuquerque region: the Treaty of Guadalupe Hidalgo in 1848 and the Compromise of 1850.

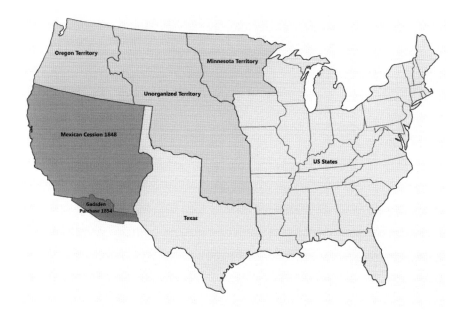

Map showing territory gained in Treaty of Guadalupe Hidalgo. *Paul Zimmerman compilation.*

The Treaty of Guadalupe Hidalgo was signed by Mexico and the United States on February 2, 1848. In this treaty, Mexico ceded the territory of Santa Fe de Nuevo México to the United States and agreed that the Rio Grande was the national border between the two countries. This meant that the State of Texas had claim to the land east of the Rio Grande. The lands west of the Rio Grande were considered part of the Mexican Cession. In total, the treaty gave the United States its goal of occupying the territory westward to the Pacific Ocean.

After the Treaty of Guadalupe Hidalgo, New Mexico residents were restless and busy trying to establish their own territory. They did not like the separation in the state at the Rio Grande, which put some citizens as Texans and others as part of the Mexican Cession. They lobbied Congress for a change to a territory or even a state.

On September 9, 1850, Congress reached an important decision in what was called the Compromise of 1850. The Texas and New Mexico Act established northern and western boundaries for Texas and established the New Mexico and Utah territories. The compromise paid Texas $10 million for the land taken from it to establish the new territory of New Mexico. The new eastern boundary for the territory was moved from the

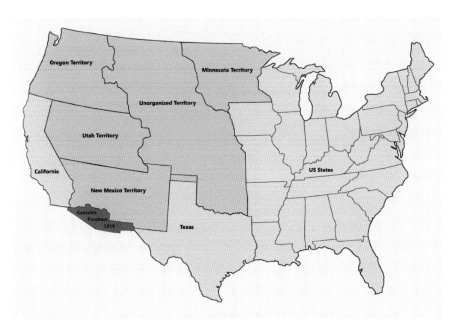

Map showing New Mexico Territory after Compromise of 1850. *Paul Zimmerman compilation.*

Rio Grande to the 103$^{rd}$ meridian. This change in boundaries picked up the Hispanic population with roots in Santa Fe de Nuevo México.

## Plaza for Acceptance of the Americans
303 Romero Street NW
Albuquerque, NM 87104
5205-221-6490

The response of Albuquerque to the American occupation was memorable. Early in September 1846, General Kearny and a cavalcade of seven hundred men traveled to Albuquerque for the first time. Albuquerque was stretched to the north some seven or eight miles, with ranches and farmhouses that were clustered thickly together. It was difficult to get to the plaza because of the large group of farms.

As the Americans marched toward Albuquerque, the crowd of settlers and curiosity-seekers swelled into the hundreds. Eventually, the long lines of Kearny's men followed by artillery and the baggage train formed ranks on the plaza in front of the San Felipe de Neri Church. There was much cheering and noise. Members of the Albuquerque militia, positioned on the flat roof of the church, fired a twenty-gun salute using old Spanish muskets. The whole affair took on the air of a Fourth of July frolic. Nowhere was there the slightest sign of hostility. The people received the soldiers kindly and seemed pleased with the change of governments and the idea of being considered as citizens of the United States. With these demonstrations of friendship, Kearny rose before the assembled populace and administered the oath of allegiance to the United States government. Henceforth, Albuquerqueans were considered to be American citizens, and those who didn't like that status could leave the country. It should be pointed out that some communities north of Santa Fe opposed the American occupation. The United States–appointed governor was killed, and there was armed resistance for a short period early in 1847.

The plaza had been created by the Spanish government and used by the Mexican government to celebrate events, and events now became the site for integration of citizens of Albuquerque into the United States.

## Quartermaster Depot for the Region
South and East of Old Town Plaza

The transformation of government from Mexico to the United States in 1846 brought about significant changes and economic opportunities for the region. A significant issue was the Native American population. During the first half of the century, there was an unofficial war going on between the Navajos and the New Mexicans. The wealthy landowners sponsored battle-hardened *caballeros* to live out west of Albuquerque for the purpose of deterring the Navajos from raids. One of their functions was to seize Navajo prisoners who could be sold as servants for five hundred pesos apiece to wealthy landowners. The Navajos had a different plan. Besides raiding farms and ranches and stealing sheep, cattle, mules and horses, they would grab youngsters, adopt them and put them to work herding sheep. Often, these captives would grow up in the Navajo culture and function as Navajos. In both cases there was intermarriage, and descendants of these two groups would have mixed heritages. Needless to say, the raiding activities fueled strong emotions.

The U.S. government took the threats of the raids of the Native Americans seriously. Starting in 1850, when New Mexico went from being under military control to being a U.S. territory, the U.S. Army studied the problem and decided to build forts at select locations in the region. Fort Union was started in 1851 to address the problems on the Santa Fe Trail with the Comanches and other Plains Indians. Fort Defiance, now in Arizona but in the New Mexico Territory until 1863, was started in 1851 to create a military presence in the Navajo region. Fort Craig was started in 1853. The United States built other temporary forts in the region starting in 1849 to deter attacks from both Navajos and Apaches on the El Camino Real.

The U.S. Army needed to supply these forts, and this became the role for Albuquerque. In 1852, Colonel Edwin Vose Sumner established Albuquerque as the nerve center for all military operations in the territory and the primary supply depot for the satellite forts erected on the southern and western fronts. A garrison was attached to the depot in Albuquerque, and this contributed to the local economy. Soldiers were used to repel raiding Indians and provide escort services for travelers and freight wagons moving in and out of the region. The depot provided civilian jobs, and these people rented quarters. The Old Town Plaza served as a parade ground for U.S. infantry and cavalry units. The depot was in existence until 1867.

The plaza continued to be the center of town life and was several acres larger in area than today. It extended farther to the east and to the south and nearly reached Railroad (Central) Avenue. Twelve military buildings—consisting of a hospital, shops, storehouses and stables—were in this extended region to the south and east.

## Bernalillo County Seat

1 Civic Plaza NW
Albuquerque, NM 87102
505-468-1290 | https://www.bernco.gov

Bernalillo County provides governance to the lands outside incorporated bodies. The county provides a sheriff and is the enforcer of the state's legal system. It maintains roads and highways in the unincorporated areas, as well at other infrastructure-type operations.

Bernalillo County was created after the Compromise of 1850. Nine counties were formed in the New Mexico Territory that went some six hundred miles from Texas to California. The map here shows the changes of boundaries from 1852 to 1903, when the boundary became stabilized. In 1852, the county is shown to have its main body near

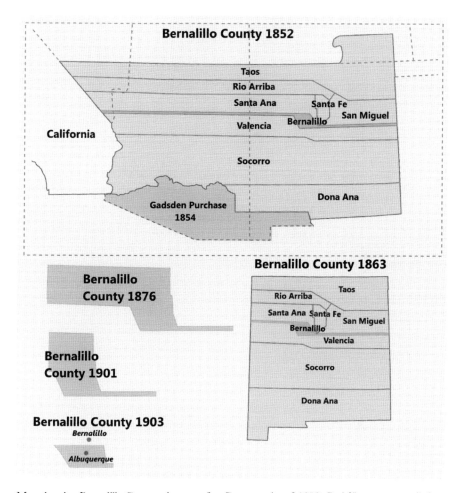

Map showing Bernalillo County changes after Compromise of 1850. *Paul Zimmerman compilation.*

Bernalillo, and then it had narrow strips of land going from the central area in both directions—to California on the west and Texas on the east. This configuration lasted until 1863, when the Arizona Territory was established and the long and narrow extension into that territory was removed. The boundaries remained stable until 1876, when Santa Ana County was dissolved and became part of Bernalillo County. McKinley County came into existence in 1901, and this new county removed the western part of the expanded Bernalillo County. The next change in the county structure occurred in 1903, when Sandoval County was taken out of the original Santa Ana acreage. With this change, the town of

Bernalillo was no longer in Bernalillo County. Also, the extension of Bernalillo County to the east was truncated in 1903.

The net effect of these changes is that Bernalillo was removed from Bernalillo County in 1903. Bernalillo became the county seat of the new Sandoval County at that time. It should be noted that there is a small deviation in the southern boundary of the post-1903 Bernalillo County line that is not shown on the map.

The county seat was moved quite often in its first twenty-four years. Records show that the town of Bernalillo housed the circuit court for the region starting in 1849. The territorial legislature moved the county seat to Los Ranchos de Albuquerque in 1851. In 1854, the legislature transferred the seat to private quarters in Old Town Albuquerque. Ambrosio Armijo's Adobe hacienda served as the county headquarters until 1878. During the period of 1878–83, the county seat was returned to the town of Bernalillo. The seat was returned to Albuquerque in 1883, and it has stayed here since.

## County Seal
Displayed on Doors of County Vehicles

Bernalillo County seal. *Courtesy of Bernalillo County.*

A Bernalillo County seal was created in the 1920s to highlight the county's heritage. The original seal had three separate parts within the circles that defined the county: a cross with the Spanish version of "With this we overcome," mountains to highlight the nearby Sandias and Manzanos and eight sheep grazing in a valley representing the original eight Spanish land grants that composed the county: Pajarito, Alameda, San Pedro, Elena Gallegos, Los Padillas, Antonio Sedillo, Atrisco and Chilili. The large cross symbolized the influence of the church in the early settlement of New Mexico. In 1985, a lawsuit was filed challenging the display of a cross on a county symbol as an unacceptable display of religion. The lawsuit was successfully supported by the U.S. Supreme Court in 1986, and the county elected to substitute the Zia sun symbol for the cross and the religious saying.

The Zia symbol was selected to commemorate the county's Native American heritage. The symbol originated with the Indians of the Zia Pueblo in ancient times. To the Zias, the four arms symbolize different events. In one sense, the arms identify the four seasons. In another, they represent a day with sunrise, noon, evening and night. Finally, the arms represent life with four divisions of childhood, youth, adulthood and old age. Everything is bound together in a circle of life and love that is without beginning and without end.

# CIVIL WAR IMPACT

The plaza that recognized the American troops in 1846 took on another role in 1862. Prior to the occupation by the Confederates, the Civil War caused tremendous disruption in the military commands in New Mexico because military officers had to decide which side they were on. Colonel Loring was the ranking officer in the Territory of New Mexico, and he joined the South. Major James Longstreet, who went on to become one of the foremost Confederate generals, was the quartermaster at Albuquerque. Major Edward R.S. Canby was promoted to colonel and entrusted to be the Union department commander for the territory. He was stationed in Fort Defiance, Arizona.

Colonel Henry Hopkins Sibley was the commander of Fort Union with a mission to protect the Santa Fe Trail. He resigned his commission and went to Texas to become a Confederate brigadier general with the goal to lead an invasion force, called the Army of New Mexico, on a quest to take possession of the territory, where he could launch assaults into Colorado and California. He would be opposing Colonel Canby. Before the war, Colonel Sibley had been a junior officer to Colonel Canby, and they were at the U.S. Military Academy at the same time. They knew each other quite well.

In late January 1862, Brigadier General Sibley and the Army of New Mexico departed from his headquarters in El Paso into the Territory of New Mexico. Colonel Edward Canby was tasked with the responsibility to lead the New Mexico forces in defending the territory.

Canby anticipated such an invasion and had tried to shore up his fighting forces with a volunteer infantry and cavalry paid and equipped by the U.S. government. Kit Carson commanded the First Regiment of New Mexico Volunteers, and Colonel Miguel Pino and Lieutenant Colonel Manuel Chaves commanded the second.

Sibley expected to meet Canby's forces at the Federal stronghold at Fort Craig south of Socorro. He decided to avoid battle at the fort and detoured around it. This drew Canby's larger force from the safety of the fort. They met at Valverde north of the fort. In the end, the Confederates won. The Union soldiers broke and ran, which caused the volunteers, many of them poorly trained, to flee in panic. They took refuge in the fort. General Sibley, not wanting to attack the fort, ordered his forces to continue their march north.

When Colonel Canby realized that Fort Craig was being bypassed, he became concerned for the military stores at the Albuquerque quartermaster depot. He sent his quartermaster, Major James Donaldson, to slip through the lines and warn the small forces in Albuquerque and Santa Fe to remove or destroy the supplies stored in both places.

Albuquerque was defenseless, and New Mexico territorial governor Connelly advised ranchers and small farmers to gather their sheep and cattle and conceal them in the Manzano Mountains. The citizens collected their valuables and took them out of town or buried them. In Albuquerque, Captain Herbert M. Enos, the assistant quartermaster and ranking officer, moved as many supplies as possible from the military depot and destroyed the rest. Enos had to burn a number of the buildings that had military equipment, along with neighboring stables and corrals.

The approaching Confederates saw three columns of smoke rising over the town with sinking spirits. They were cold and hungry, and their horses were thin from fast marching and short supplies of grass.

When Sibley arrived on March 6, he moved into the adobe home of Rafael Armijo and his younger brother, Manuel, who were supporters of the Confederate cause. This home became Sibley's headquarters in Old Town. The brothers were nephews of former governor Manuel Armijo. The store owners turned over $200,000 in goods for Confederate script, which later turned out to be worthless. General Sibley found some Southern sympathizers in the nearby communities and eventually gathered enough supplies to last his army for about three months.

The Confederates marched north with the goal of capturing Fort Union. At the same time, Colonel Canby had appealed to Colorado and California governors for assistance. A group of Colorado volunteers under Major John Chivington did a forced march south to Fort Union to shore up the thin Union forces in New Mexico and discourage an invasion of their state.

The two armies met at Glorieta Pass, which was a major pass between Las Vegas and Santa Fe, and the Confederates won the direct conflict. Some of the Union forces, led by Lieutenant Colonel Manuel Chaves, slipped behind the Confederate lines and burned sixty-one wagons in Sibley's supply train. This was a devastating blow to General Sibley, and his troops had no choice but to start a retreat.

## Battle of Albuquerque
Artillery Exchange between Barelas and Old Town

The Confederate troops retreated to Santa Fe and then to Albuquerque. A small group of the Confederates camped in the region of Laguna and Railroad (Central) Avenues. On April 8, Canby, then with a small portion of his army, which was located at the small farming settlement of Barelas, ordered four small cannons to fire on the Confederates. There was open space between the armies. The cannons of the Confederates returned the artillery fire. The artillery-only battle lasted for several hours; there were no casualties. A worried group of citizens approached Canby and told

Replicas of guns used by Confederates in 1862 in Battle of Albuquerque. *Roger Zimmerman Collection.*

him that the Confederates were not letting women and children, who had remained in their homes, leave and find a safe refuge. Canby ordered his men to stop firing. The Battle of Albuquerque thus ended near nightfall without any impact to the population.

Canby was worried that a larger group of Confederate soldiers would arrive and decided to sneak away during the night. He left his musicians playing while he departed to the south with the remainder of his troops. The ploy worked. Canby moved into the Sandias, where the victorious Colorado volunteers joined him, and together they headed back to Albuquerque.

Sibley, who had been residing in Santa Fe at the start of the retreat, arrived in Albuquerque and assessed the situation. They had food for fifteen days and only thirty-five to forty rounds of ammunition per man. Sibley and the officers agreed on retreat to Texas on April 12. This retreat ended the Confederate initiative into the capturing of New Mexico, Colorado and California.

In the retreat, the Confederates buried eight brass howitzer cannons in a corral behind the San Felipe de Neri Church. They were later recovered, and two are preserved at the Albuquerque Museum. Replicas of the cannons are displayed on the east side of the plaza.

## Five Flags Over Old Town Plaza
303 Romero Street NW
Albuquerque, NM 87104
5205-221-6490

The Albuquerque Planning Department undertook a project to install five flags on the Old Town Plaza on July 13, 1969. The goal was to display flags from the governments that had governed New Mexico. It was commonly accepted that the governments were the United States, Spain, Mexico, Texas and the Confederate States of America.

The big question mark was Texas because Texans had never actually occupied the Albuquerque region. The Republic of Texas claimed the Rio Grande as its western boundary when it was formed in 1836. The U.S. Army produced a map of the Southwest in 1844 showing this configuration. Texas became a U.S. state in 1845. As late as 2016, the Daughters of the Republic of Texas asked the Albuquerque Historical Society to help establish a marker in Albuquerque to commemorate this status. After a research effort by the Albuquerque Historical Society was

Five flags flying over Old Town Plaza. *Roger Zimmerman Collection.*

produced, this request was rescinded. This Texas claim for the Rio Grande boundary was not accepted by the U.S. Congress when statehood for Texas was established in 1845, but this was not common knowledge. Thus, five flagpoles were erected instead of four, and they still exist.

At the planned dedication ceremony in 1969, the Rio Grande Lions Club was to present five flags to the city. A number of local historians and Old Town residents immediately rose in protest. Texas had never occupied the eastern half of New Mexico or raised its flag over Albuquerque's Plaza. The Rio Grande Lions Club agreed to the changes and substituted the New Mexico flag for the Texas flag. Some Texans had been invited to bring a flag to the dedication and then were disinvited after the hubbub.

The five flags of Spain, Mexico, the United States, New Mexico and the Confederacy flew over the plaza from 1969 until 2015, when there were protests about the Confederate flag. Mayor Richard Berry ordered the removal of that flag. The discussion of the removal of the Confederate flag can be found in newspaper articles of that year. The flag of the City of Albuquerque is flown in its stead.

It should be pointed out that one individual has raised and lowered these flags for the past forty-five years. James Hoffsis, Korean War veteran and co-owner of Treasure House Books & Gifts, which is located on the south side of the Old Town Plaza, has purchased the flags over this period and kept them flying.

The flags are located on the west side of the Old Town Plaza. Underneath the five flags are four brass plaques that summarize Albuquerque history through the railroad era. The plaques (including their wording) were promoted and created by the Albuquerque Historical Society and were funded by Woodmen of the World, Plaza Business Association, Albuquerque Historical Society and the Kiwanis Club of Albuquerque.

# ENTER THE RAILROAD IN 1880

The establishment of the Atchison, Topeka and Santa Fe (AT&SF) Railway in Albuquerque, commonly known as the Santa Fe Railway, took some interesting turns. Albuquerque wasn't the first selection for the main terminal.

Railroad construction, which had started between two towns in Kansas, Atchison and Topeka, went westward, and by the summer of 1878, it had reached Trinidad, Colorado. Under some complex financial arrangements, the final result was that the AT&SF would build track to the Middle Valley of the Rio Grande, and then the track would be laid west toward the Pacific under the Atlantic and Pacific (A&P) name. Under this arrangement, a highly desired transcontinental railroad could be established, and later the AT&SF would become the final railroad name.

The AT&SF entered New Mexico in 1878 under somewhat of a cloud. It was laying track faster than it could be properly financed. The company had to scrimp to meet payrolls and bills. As the railroad tracks approached Las Vegas, "The railroad wanted an outright gift of $10,000, a free right of way, thirty free acres of ground for a depot, and one-half interest in 400 acres of land for a suburb addition to Las Vegas," as historian Marc Simmons has noted. This demand was not what Las Vegas citizens were anticipating. They were thinking of railroad traffic coming to the community and local citizens benefiting financially. The citizens were unwilling to meet these financial demands, and the railroad depot, yards, shop and roundhouse were built about a mile from the plaza. Las Vegas had the important role of being the staging area for the track construction westward through the Sangre de Cristo Mountains, and a new community developed around the railroad depot and yards.

The next major community for the track layers was Santa Fe. In 1878, the community of Santa Fe was negotiating with officials from the Denver and Rio Grande (D&RG) Railway, which was planning a railroad from Colorado down through the middle of New Mexico. They also came to Santa Fe with their hands out. Citizens would have to pay for the privilege of having the north–south rail service. There was opposition. Santa Feans also knew that there was an east–west track coming from Las Vegas. It wasn't clear just where the track would be laid, but after all, it was named after their city. Certainly, they would be on the east–west route.

In 1879, the D&RG shelved plans for expansion into northern New Mexico, and this took Santa Fe off the hook for that commitment. Meanwhile, the AT&SF officials had a dilemma: should they go through Santa Fe or should they take a better route and make faster progress toward reaching the Pacific? In the end, they decided that advancing toward the coast had the most priority and offered to construct a spur from the main line up to Santa Fe if the citizens would pay for the spur. Santa Feans decided that they wanted rail service and voted to approve bonds for the spur construction from Lamy.

The main line of the AT&SF was going over Glorieta Pass and through the Galisteo Basin. The AT&SF officials were looking for a depot, offices, extensive yards and a good place to cross the Rio Grande. Bernalillo looked like a good spot, so the railroad arranged a meeting with Lewis Kingman, chief surveyor; Albert Robinson, chief engineer; and Don Jose Leandro Perea, owner of extensive land in and around Bernalillo. The railroad officials wanted a right-of-way through Don Jose's vast acreage of land on the outskirts of Bernalillo for the offices and yards. They offered to pay the going price of $2 to $3 per acre for what they wanted. Don Jose told the railroad that if they wanted this land, they would have to pay $425 per acre. Kingman and Robinson rolled up their maps and returned to the stage station and were soon seen headed south toward Albuquerque. Bernalillo was not going to be a major stop on the railroad.

Obviously, Don Jose didn't want the railroad yards in his backyard. He had wide ranching interests, mercantile establishments and a freighting operation. Some think that he was afraid of long-haul competition in the freight business. If he was, he was short-sighted because he didn't realize the opportunities for short-haul opportunities that would come with the railroad. Bernalillo's loss was Albuquerque's gain.

The location of the railroad through the Albuquerque portion of the Middle Valley was driven largely by geography. With the loss of Bernalillo as a crossing point of the Rio Grande, the next-best place was about twelve miles south of Albuquerque, near Isleta Pueblo. The AT&SF would construct the line to there, cross the river and then make a fork. One branch would go west toward California under the A&P name, while the other would go south to El Paso on the west side of the river as the AT&SF. The bend in the Rio Grande and the location of Old Town Albuquerque near the river precluded the tracks reaching the plaza because a straight alignment between Bernalillo and the Isleta fork would go on the east side without going through the floodplain. The tracks were to be laid on slightly higher ground just east of the old Rio Grande riverbed. This was near where one branch of El Camino Real went.

Three forward-thinking men were mainly responsible for having the railroad yards, offices, depot and roundhouse located in Albuquerque: Franz Huning, William Hazeldine and Elias Stover. These individuals are examples of how Albuquerque benefited from the migration of talented and enterprising individuals over the Santa Fe Trail.

Franz Huning was born in Germany in 1827 and immigrated to the United States in 1848. He arrived in what was to become the Territory of New Mexico in 1849 and went to work in Albuquerque in 1852. In 1857, he opened his own store in partnership with his brother, Charles. The Hunings purchased wagons and brought goods to Albuquerque along the Santa Fe Trail. William Hazeldine was born and educated in Arkansas, where in his twenties he had been a state legislator and a district judge. He came to Albuquerque in 1877 and set up a law practice. Elias Stover came to Albuquerque in 1876 looking for opportunities associated with railroad building. He had been a lieutenant governor of Kansas in 1872–74 and had seen the opportunities that would come with the railroad. He became a merchant on the plaza. In later years, he would become the first president of the University of New Mexico. These three gentlemen were exceptional people who fortunately found one another and started the operations in anticipation of Albuquerque becoming a railroad center.

Word got to Albuquerque about the city-railroad negotiations in Las Vegas, Santa Fe and Bernalillo, and there was some apprehension about what would happen. In June 1879, railroad officials met with landowners to see if they could get a right-of-way up to two hundred feet in width. Community leaders met and decided that they wanted rail service, and they were inclined to do whatever was needed to get the AT&SF terminal and rail yards located on the east side of the valley. In January 1880, Chief Engineer

Albert Robinson made the formal announcement that the AT&SF would build its depot and yards on the east side of the valley. They just needed to work out the details.

Franz Huning was at the head of the pack in trying to secure the railroad facilities in Albuquerque. He was quietly buying land south and east of the plaza and had acquired about seven hundred acres. He took the lead in establishing a road between Old Town Albuquerque and the new depot, which was to be called Railroad Avenue.

Next came an interesting financial arrangement. In March 1880, Franz Huning, William Hazeldine and Elias Stover formed the New Mexico Town Company. The town company was a subsidiary of the New Mexico and Southern Pacific Railroad Company, which was an auxiliary of the AT&SF. This meant that the AT&SF would own the property of the town company. The three partners in the town company bought 3.1 square miles of land at modest prices and deeded the property to the New Mexico Town Company for one dollar.

This is where the financial arrangements got interesting. More land had been collected by the town company than was needed for the railroad tracks, depot and shops. The arrangement was that the railroad could sell excess land through the town company promotions, and the trio of agents would get half of the profits for these sales. This means that the railroad and the operators of the town company would each get revenue from real estate sales. These three knew that the railroad would increase the value of the land and that, even at 50 percent of the revenue, they would benefit financially—and they did. This was a good situation for Albuquerque, as relations between the community and the railroad were good. The railroad got its land for essentially nothing and could make some profit, and the three risk-takers were financially rewarded as well.

Bernalillo's loss was Albuquerque's gain for the second time in less than two hundred years.

## Wheels Museum in Railroad Facilities

1100 Second Street SW
Albuquerque, NM 87102
505-243-6269

The railroad shops that emerged from the decision to locate the yards in Albuquerque is a testament to the foresight that the trio of founders probably underestimated. As it turned out, the AT&SF selected Albuquerque to be one of four major maintenance facilities, the others being in Topeka, Kansas; Cleburne, Texas; and San Bernardino, California.

The shops and yard were located in the community of Barelas about one mile south of the depot. The railway shops were the largest employer in the city during the railroad's heyday. The shops employed about 1,000 in the 1920s, expanding to a peak of 1,500 in the 1940s.

The first buildings to be completed in the 1800s were the roundhouse, storehouse, power station and freight car shops, and they were demolished in the early 1900s. The shops were expanded in 1915–25 to consist of eighteen buildings on twenty-seven acres, and all are still standing, although in serious disrepair. The facilities are in the National Register of Historic Places.

Currently, the Wheels Museum is located in the railyard facilities. The museum is dedicated to collecting, preserving and creating educational exhibits about the history of transportation in Albuquerque and New Mexico, with an emphasis on the impact of the development of the area. The collections embrace the history of the railroads and the impact of the rail yards on Albuquerque, as well as automobiles, horse and wagon and other modes of transportation.

View of Santa Fe Railroad repair facility, circa 1980. *Albuquerque Museum, 1982.043.02, Richard A. Bice Collection.*

## New Town Post Office Location
Original Building at Railroad Avenue and Third Street SW

The United States Post Office discovered a problem when the railroad came. It had an established community called Albuquerque, and with the addition of the railroad and surrounding townsite some two miles away, it was in a dilemma about what to do. Where should mail be delivered and picked up? On February 10, 1881, it issued a charter establishing a post office in New Town. The new office was on Third Street across from the Armijo House on Railroad Avenue. The problem was that letters addressed to Albuquerque could go to the office on the Old Town Plaza or the new one on Third Street. One plan by the post office was to close the plaza post office down, but people living there couldn't accept that the railroad town, less than two years old, should get the priority for a post office. After all, they had been there since 1706. After much consternation, the post office suggested that the plaza post office be called Armijo, since that was the dominant family in Old Town, and the new site be called Albuquerque. That didn't work either.

Finally, in 1886, the post office called the plaza station Old Albuquerque and the Third Street station New Albuquerque. This designation was accepted, and most people called the two regions Old Town and New Town. New Albuquerque was incorporated in 1885. As a general rule of thumb, New Town was used for most descriptions of New Albuquerque, while the latter was used for mailings and formal documents. Albuquerque was incorporated as a city in 1891 with a mayor city council form of government. An 1891 Sanborn map of the region shows Albuquerque and Old Albuquerque as the major communities.

## Original Townsite
Established with Railroad Avenue as the Main Artery

The emerging community near the railroad depot was unincorporated during its first five years. The New Mexico Town Company was focused on land development and did not provide the incoming citizens with any form of government. The prime real estate surrounding the tracks, known as the "original townsite," was developed by the New Mexico Town Company under the leadership of Franz Huning, William Hazeldine and Elias Stover.

They started the process by laying out the 3.1 square miles that constituted the original townsite. Colonel Walter G. Marmon, a civil

72

engineer, was available, and they hired him to lay out and name new streets. He used the scheme where streets running north and south between the railroad and the border of Old Town were called First through Sixteenth. Streets east of the tracks were named for the Franz Huning family: Arno, Edith and Walter Streets. High Street was next because it ran through the elevated hills bounding the valley and was thought to be as far east as people would want to live. The major east–west thoroughfare between the depot and Old Town had already been named Railroad Avenue by Franz Huning. Colonel Marmon named the east–west thoroughfares, called avenues, after minerals and fuel: Copper, Gold, Silver, Lead and Coal. Copper was to the north and the remainder to the south of Railroad Avenue. The three avenues south of Coal were named Huning, Hazeldine and Stover. The reason for the predominance of the avenues south of Railroad Avenue was the forthcoming presence of the railway yards and shops along the tracks.

Colonel Marmon also established wards for the four quadrants of Albuquerque, with the intersection of Railroad Avenue and the AT&SF railway as the center. The wards were identified by directions (e.g., the NE ward was the region to the north of Railroad Avenue and east of the tracks). This distinction would become important when voting and school districts were established. Railroad Avenue became Central Avenue in 1908. There was some confusion in this renaming, as Marc Simmons reported it as occurring in 1912. In a renaming of the Albuquerque streets in 1952, all addresses were identified with the quadrant identification included.

## New Town Center

*Original Building Located between Gold and Silver Avenues on Second Street SW*

Citizens recognized the need for governmental structure and initiated actions to improve the viability of a growing community. Initially, they filled the gap by forming a county precinct and electing a constable and justice of the peace on February 1, 1881. One year later, local businessmen got involved in business matters by creating a board of trade. The group was composed of leading merchants and professional men who were interested in developing New Town. The board established a Merchants' Police Force to maintain order and developed a means to tax merchants for funds to pay for municipal projects. Their policy was to raise revenues by assessing merchants for "voluntary contributions."

In 1884, sometime sheriff Santiago Baca and William Hazeldine, along with a young lawyer newly arrived in town, Harvey B. Fergusson, spearheaded a drive for incorporation. On July 28, 1884, Grant's Opera House hosted a public meeting, which led to the securing of a town charter and the issuance of a call for an election to incorporate. In balloting on June 4, 1885, New Towners approved the action almost four to one. The board of trade would become the board of trustees. At a follow-up election on July 4, a German-born merchant named Henry N. Jaffa, who was a leader in the Jewish community, became Albuquerque's first mayor. Jaffa had previously served as president of the board of trade.

With Jaffa, four trustees were elected to constitute a municipal government board. All were small businessmen, and none had held positions of prominence before. They came from the four wards. Indications are that they had come to office with the approval of people like Huning, Hazeldine and Stover. The town charter called for the board of trustees to obtain municipal funds through sales of business licenses. This gave the board structure for revenue generation that it didn't have with the earlier voluntary contributions. Saloonkeepers paid the largest fee for a license and bond. Charges to hotel managers, shop owners and professional men were smaller.

The board of trustees was empowered to pass municipal ordinances. The first ones were concerned with regulation of dance halls, gambling dens and saloons. It also granted franchises to utility companies. The board had the authorization to float bond issues, which could be used for development of sewers, a fire department and street development and maintenance. By 1890, most of the streets in the business district had been graded, guttered and lined with boardwalks.

The territorial legislature passed a new law in 1890 allowing larger towns to reincorporate as cities, to be governed by mayors and aldermen. An election for this new status was conducted in April 1891, and it passed by a large majority. New Albuquerque, with a population of 3,785, continued to be divided into four wards, each ward having the right to elect two aldermen to a city council. Old Town remained as a separate community until integration into Albuquerque in 1949. As it turned out, New Town continued growing and prospering, while Old Town declined in importance as the new activities were centered on the railroad.

## Wool Warehouse
516 First Street NW
Albuquerque, NM 87102

New Albuquerque soon had a diverse economy that was built around the railroad. Sheep raising and the wool trade were the dominant economic drivers in the latter half of the nineteenth century. Albuquerque's convenient location in the midst of sheep country and its excellent marketing, processing and shipping facilities soon made it the focal point of wool trade. As early as October 1880, local merchants shipped away forty freight cars of wool and hides, some of it brought from as far away as eastern Arizona. People in the valley operated the Rio Grande Woolen Mills, which gave employment to carders, spinners and weavers. The mills manufactured fabrics, and tailors and seamstresses produced garments for men and women. These activities produced a cash flow into the region and also provided blankets and clothing to the local citizens without the added transportation costs.

Albuquerque's central location and convenient access to the Santa Fe Railway made it the hub of the New Mexico wool trade, which flourished as American demand for wool increased rapidly after World War I. The Wool

Wool Warehouse, built in 1929. *Norman Falk, photographer.*

Warehouse was built in 1929 on a spur of the railway so that goods could be easily shipped and received. The warehouse is a symbol of the early sheep trade. The industry grew in the early part of the twentieth century, and a building was constructed to house the goods. The building had the capacity to store 5 million pounds of wool and hides.

The warehouse is in the National Register of Historic Places. The facility currently houses Youth Development Inc.

## Mule-Drawn Trolley
Rails at Unique Intersection: Central Avenue and Fourth Street

There was an early recognition that there needed to be good transportation between the railroad station and Old Town. The Street Railway Company, incorporated late in 1880, was formed to provide local railroad service to residents. This was an important transportation link over the nearly two miles between these two communities and was a symbol of the acceptance of each community to each other. Within a year, eight mule-drawn cars and three miles of track connected Elias Stover's house, near the plaza, with New Town and the suburb of Barelas, where the railroad shops were located. Stores were constructed along Railroad Avenue and First Street. Growth of New Town merchants was directed along Railroad Avenue toward Old Town. Many of the merchants lived in Old Town and commuted to New Town on the trolley. Workers at the railroad shops in Barelas used the trolley to commute to and from work as well.

Huning and Hazeldine were among the founders of the trolley, but the president was Oliver A. Cromwell, a New Yorker who arrived in 1879 and began investing in real estate. He saw an opportunity and made it happen. The trolley operation continued until 1904, when cars became powered with electricity from overhead power lines. This lasted until the late 1920s, when bus transportation took over.

The light, narrow-gauge tracks ran down the center of Railroad Avenue on an elevated grade that varied from a few inches to two feet. The street was a stretch of loose sand and dust during dry weather and a quagmire of mud when it rained. A sidewalk was created by nailing planks to the ties between the rails from First Street to the Armijo House at Railroad and Third Street. In early years, two mules were used to pull the trolleys, and in the 1890s, the system was changed and a single horse was used for each car. The later cars were light and were known to blow over in heavy winds.

Horse-drawn trolley on Railroad Avenue. *Albuquerque Museum, 1982.180.277, Dr. John Airy Collection.*

Two rails are visibly embedded in the pavement surface at the unique intersection. These rails commemorate this important contribution to early Albuquerque development.

## Alvarado Hotel
Site at First Street and Railroad Avenue SW

The railroad depot soon became the focal point for transit in and out of Albuquerque. The Alvarado Hotel was built in 1902 to provide lodging and food immediately next to the railway station. The hotel was built as a complex that included the train depot, a Fred Harvey restaurant, an Indian arts shop

77

with curio museum and a large open area opening onto the platform for people getting on and off the trains. All were owned by the AT&SF, but the hotel and restaurant were run by Fred Harvey as part of the Harvey House chain. The complex was designed by architect Charles Whittlesey in the California Mission style and featured roofs with red tiles. The interior was designed by Mary J. Colter using regional artifacts and Indian motifs. The old Indian curio store was made of poured reinforced concrete in 1912. This building still exists.

The hotel was named for Hernando de Alvarado, Coronado's lieutenant, who led the first scouting party into the Middle Valley in 1540. The hotel contained seventy-five guest rooms, a large lobby, two parlors, a reading room and a barbershop. It had the convenience of electric lights. The hotel was at the heart of the city. People went to promenade and gathered to watch celebrities. Many weddings and ladies' lunches were held there. The famous Harvey Girls worked the grill.

The hotel was torn down in 1970 after a failed effort by the city to purchase it and has been rebuilt to be used by the City of Albuquerque as the Alvarado Transportation Center (ATC), a multimodal transit hub located at 100 First Street SW, which is in downtown Albuquerque. The ATC was designed to be reminiscent of the Alvarado Hotel. Now the center serves the Albuquerque bus system, Amtrak trains and Greyhound bus lines. It also serves as a hub for the New Mexico Rail Runner commuter rail line.

The coming of the railroad also signaled the opportunity for the mobility of politicians so they could interact better with the populace. Two U.S. presidents, Theodore Roosevelt and William Taft, made important visits to Albuquerque in the early days. Their activities were centered at the Alvarado.

President Theodore Roosevelt visited Albuquerque on May 5, 1903. He made an address to an estimated fifteen thousand citizens on First Street in front of the Alvarado Hotel. New Mexico was thirsting for statehood, and the pressure was on the president to sign the necessary legislation. The president's podium overlooked a large elevated tableau, which had forty-five girls standing with signs indicating the existing states. Oklahoma hadn't been admitted in 1903. A little girl held a sign with New Mexico on it and stood in front of the others with hands extended appealing for admission of New Mexico. The president spoke for a few minutes and mentioned the need for more irrigation in the territory to help the statehood application. He made a short trip to downtown and then departed later in the day. He

Roosevelt statehood arch for downtown parade, 1903. *Albuquerque Museum, 1982.081.036.*

President Taft in reviewing stand at Alvarado, 1909. *Albuquerque Museum, 2008.15.2, David Kelsey Collection.*

was presented with a Navajo rug woven by a Navajo woman working at the Indian store in the Alvarado.

President William Howard Taft visited Albuquerque on October 15, 1909. The visit was headquartered at the Alvarado Hotel. There were about five to six thousand people in attendance. The president spoke for about fifteen minutes and delivered a pledge to secure statehood for New Mexico. He attended an all-male reception and dinner that evening and later joined a women's ball and stayed until midnight. President Taft signed the statehood bill on August 21, 1911, and New Mexico became the forty-seventh state on January 6, 1912.

## Santa Fe Locomotive no. 2926
City Park at Intersection of Eighth Street and Haines Avenue NW

Albuquerque has active railroad historians. The New Mexico Steam Locomotive and Railroad Historical Society is located in Albuquerque and has a project to restore AT&SF locomotive no. 2926 to operating condition. The steam locomotive was originally built in 1944 by Baldwin Locomotive Works. This locomotive was part of the last group of steam passenger locomotives built for the Santa Fe Railway. This class of locomotives, 2900, was the heaviest 4-8-4 built in the United States. The last run was in 1953. The locomotive and

Santa Fe locomotive no. 2926. *Historic Albuquerque Inc., City of Albuquerque Collection.*

caboose were donated to the City of Albuquerque in 1956 in recognition of the city's 250th anniversary. The locomotive and caboose were initially placed in Coronado Park at Second Street and I-40 for public display.

The New Mexico Steam Locomotive and Railroad Historical Society purchased the locomotive on July 26, 1999. After a few moves, the locomotive was located at the intersection of Eighth Street and Haines Avenue. The society is actively working to restore the locomotive to operating condition. As it is, it is listed in the National Register of Historic Places.

# QUALITY OF LIFE IN AN EMERGING CITY

By 1881, a building boom was well underway in what would become the business district of New Town. The earliest structures arrived on railroad cars. These structures could be easily taken apart, moved or removed. The railroad made it possible to have more durable buildings. The earliest structures were replaced with more permanent buildings made out of lumber, fired brick and cut and cast stone. Iron shapes could be included in the construction process, and this made construction of multiple story buildings much more feasible.

The rapid occupation of the townsite was fueled by a combination of unique features brought on by three things: an aggressive town company, people in Old Town recognizing the opportunities that were available and a townsite that was spacious and inviting.

A photograph was found that shows New Town in its infancy. The photograph, taken in May 1881, a little over a year after the first train arrived, shows the townsite and key features available at that time. The photo was taken from near the tracks south of Railroad Avenue and looks to the northwest. The trees in the background show the location of Old Town nearly two miles away.

The large building shown near the center is the original Armijo House in New Town. The Armijo House, perched on the southwest corner of Third Street and Railroad Avenue, was completed by Mariano Armijo, son of Ambrosio Armijo (a merchant from Old Town). It became a symbol of anticipated prosperity. The hotel was a three-story structure that had

View of Albuquerque looking northwest from railroad depot, May 1, 1881. *Albuquerque Museum, 1990.013.113, Walter Haussamen Collection.*

seventy-five rooms. The owner wanted a "city style" hotel in this new setting that would be more distinctive than the traditional adobe. The hotel had a dining room, and male patrons were expected to wear coats.

A careful examination of the photo shows a ditch in the center. This was a natural ditch that went along what was the Rio Grande channel at one time. The ditch, which originated to the northeast at a pond located east of the tracks near Martineztown, was called the "Lower Barelas Canal" by some and the "Barelas Ditch" by others. The canal went under the railroad tracks and gave relief in times of high water. The canal often had water in it and was used as a sewer during the early days of settlement. The canal joined the Rio Grande near Barelas.

With the coming of the railroad, living conditions that had existed for more than 174 years were changing. Protestants began arriving in greater numbers in the 1870s and expected to have their own religious practices. Two reverends, Jacob Mills Ashley of the Congregational Church and Nathaniel Hawthorne Gale of the Methodist Episcopal Church, came in 1879 and started congregations that became churches in 1881. Activities leading to the establishment of their churches are discussed later in the chapter.

The Episcopalians were another Protestant denomination that showed an early interest in Albuquerque. In February 1880, a separate room in the Exchange Hotel was furnished as a chapel, representing the beginnings of St. John's Episcopal Church. In 1882, the congregation acquired its own building in New Town at the corner of Fourth Street and Silver Avenue.

The Presbyterians then got into the act. The first Presbyterian congregation was formed in 1880 by assembling five members who met regularly in a private home in Old Town. Shortly afterward, Reverend James A. Menaul arrived and led a drive for construction of the first Presbyterian church in 1882 on lots given by the Town Company at Silver Avenue and Fifth Street. The Baptists chartered a church in 1887 and were followed by the Lutherans in 1891.

African Americans formed an African Methodist Episcopal Church in 1882. The congregation floated about, using temporary quarters, until a permanent church could be built in 1892 at the corner of Coal Avenue and Third Street.

Albuquerque's Jewish community went without a place of worship until 1897, when fifty families organized a congregation and laid plans for erecting a synagogue. Three years later, on September 14, 1900, the new Temple Albert, at Seventh Street and Gold Avenue, was dedicated by Rabbi Pizer Jacobs.

The Catholic Church continued to dominate religious life in Old Town, where the population remained predominantly Hispano. But in 1882, it followed the lead of the Protestants and opened the Immaculate Conception Church on Sixth Street and Copper Avenue. The new parish attracted members from the business community, the families of railroad workers and the few Hispanos who took up residence in New Town. The Catholics started private schools at this new location.

Albuquerque became a health mecca. By the early 1900s, New Mexico's sunshine, dry air, high altitude and warm climate were attracting health seekers, particularly tuberculosis (TB) patients who were "chasing the cure." By 1909, that disease had become the nation's leading cause of death.

Albuquerque boosters took advantage of the situation to promote the town as the health-seeker's haven. Albuquerque's Commercial Club, a forerunner of the chamber of commerce, promoted Albuquerque to easterners suffering from TB (or "consumption"). By 1910, tuberculars—or "lungers," as they were called—numbered three thousand out of a population of thirteen thousand. Many had arrived on stretchers. This migration of health sufferers made a significant impact on Albuquerque's economy and development and is discussed in more detail later in this chapter.

## First National Bank Building
217–233 Central Avenue NW
Albuquerque, NM 87102

Banks were needed to support a growing economy in the territory. The First National Bank of Santa Fe opened its doors in the capital on April 17, 1871, becoming the first commercial bank in the territory. The first bank in Albuquerque came in 1878 when the Central Bank was opened in a small adobe building on the southwest corner of the plaza. It was started by the Raynolds brothers, Jefferson, Frederick and Josua. In 1881, the Raynoldses began construction of a two-story brick building on the corner of Second

First National Bank building, built in 1922. *Historic Albuquerque Inc., City Planning Collection.*

Street and Gold Avenue, and as soon as it was completed, they abandoned the Old Town location to get nearer to the center of economic activity. This move was part of a coming realization that the economic patterns in Albuquerque were changing.

The Central Bank soon had a competitor. A group of wealthy Bernalillo County residents chartered the First National Bank of Albuquerque in December 1881, with Mariano S. Otero of Bernalillo, Elias S. Stover, Nicolas T. Armijo (son of Cristobal Armijo) and Cristobal Armijo as directors. Other prominent names that appeared among the founders included Franz Huning's brother, Louis; Felipe Chavez, a Belen merchant; Jose Leandro

Perea of Bernalillo (the person who rejected the railroad); and Justo Armijo. The stockholders of the new First National Bank experienced some rough times and sold out to the Raynolds brothers in 1884.

With the merger, the Raynolds brothers decided that the Central Bank should became the First National Bank of Albuquerque. The newly named bank continued to occupy the office at Second Street and Gold Avenue until 1922, when a new eight-story building was erected at Third Street and Central Avenue. It was Albuquerque's first skyscraper and is in the National Register of Historic Places.

## St. Joseph Sanitorium
601 Dr. Martin Luther King Drive NE
Albuquerque, NM 87102

By the 1880s, Albuquerque had at least two doctors but no hospital facilities. As the railroad reached Albuquerque in 1880, it created a need for treatment of injured railroad workers. In 1881, the railroad built a small hospital east of the tracks for twenty patients. This became the first hospital in Albuquerque. The hospital burned down in 1902, and patients were transferred to the St. Joseph Sanitorium.

Seeing a need for better facilities, churches established hospital facilities. The first was St. Joseph Sanitorium, opened by Sister Blandina Segale and the Sisters of Charity in 1902. The three-story brick building held patient rooms, a kitchen, a surgical ward and nursing stations. The new facility had beds for thirty patients. The Sisters' mission was to treat the poor and underserved, and they were particularly concerned about TB patients. Now the facility is part of the Lovelace Medical Center.

The Protestant churches got involved. In 1903, Reverend Hugh A. Cooper, a Presbyterian minister, came to Albuquerque to improve his health and became pastor of the First Presbyterian Church. Concerned with the large number of TB patients in the city, many destitute and dying, he decided that Presbyterians must lend a hand. In 1908, he founded the Southwestern Presbyterian Sanitorium, with support from the Commercial Club. The facility was a five-room house on Oak Street near Railroad Avenue. It was the city's second such sanitorium.

Soon the town had eight sanitoria, mostly clustered between downtown and the university. These patients provided a significant economic boost to Albuquerque, and they also became a source for some of the city's

St. Joseph's Hospital, 1902. *Historic Albuquerque Inc., Nancy Tucker Collection.*

prominent city leaders and outstanding citizens. Recovered patients who stayed included Carrie Wooster, whose then suitor, Clyde Tingley, would become the city's flamboyant mayor and New Mexico governor; John Milne, who was APS school superintendent for forty-five years; Clinton Anderson, who was a notable U.S. senator and member of Truman's cabinet; France Scholes, vice-president of the University of New Mexico; Grace Thompson Edmister, who founded and conducted the Albuquerque Civic Symphony; architect John Gaw Meem; and William R. Lovelace, who founded Lovelace Clinic.

## Journal Center
7777 Jefferson Street NE
Albuquerque, NM 87109
505-823-7000 | thejournalcenter.com

In the three decades before the turn of the nineteenth century, Albuquerque saw a number of small newspapers come and go. One stood out in the 1870s: the *Albuquerque Republican*, which was published by William McGuinness. He, along with his Hispano wife, published a bilingual weekly newspaper from a small adobe office at 202 San Felipe SW, which is in Old Town. McGuinness was a strong advocate for economic progress in Albuquerque for more than a decade and was at the forefront in supporting the selection of Albuquerque over Bernalillo for the location of the railroad depot and yards.

After the railroad came, small presses and small newspapers made their presence known. One, Albuquerque Publishing Company, survived and its heritage is discussed as the Journal Center.

Albuquerque's first daily, the *Golden Gate*, was started on June 4, 1880, but unfortunately the editor died suddenly and the press was acquired by a new company, the Albuquerque Publishing Company. The new company started publishing the *Albuquerque Daily Journal* on October 14, 1880. Franz Huning was president, and William C. Hazeldine was secretary of the company. Huning and Hazeldine lost their zest for newspaper publishing and sold the company to Tom Hughes in 1881.

The original Albuquerque Publishing Company reorganized, with Elias S. Stover as president, and repurchased the paper from Hughes in 1884. Also, the name was changed to the *Albuquerque Morning Journal*. After remaining for a while as editor and manager, Tom Hughes departed in 1887 to become co-owner and editor of another paper, the *Albuquerque Daily Citizen*.

The Albuquerque Publishing Company went through several name changes and editorial policies for the newspaper throughout its history. The

Journal Center. *Roger Zimmerman Collection.*

company settled on the *Albuquerque Journal* in 1925 with an independent editorial policy, and that continues to this day. The Albuquerque Publishing Company was merged into a larger organization called the Journal Publishing Company. The Lang family became the publishers in 1956 and have continued in that capacity since. Community outreach has become a goal of the publishing company, and in 1979, the owners wanted to set a new standard for a business setting in Albuquerque. They created the Journal Center.

The Journal Center is a campus-like environment rich with thousands of trees, shrubs and seasonal plantings mixed in with trails and streets. The center contains high-tech firms, banks, financial organizations and the Albuquerque Publishing Company. The Journal Center is an outgrowth of early newspaper publishing in the city.

## First Episcopal Methodist Church in New Town

315 Coal Avenue SW
Albuquerque, NM 87102
505-243-5646

Two reverends, Jacob Mills Ashley of the Congregational Church and Nathaniel Hawthorne Gale of the Methodist Episcopal Church, came in 1879 and started congregations. Ashley set up a church in Old Town, but he was not well received in a predominantly Catholic community and soon constructed a small, white, framed church at the corner of Broadway and Coal Avenue. The building was in the east highlands, outside the New Town townsite, on a lot donated by Franz Huning. The small church was completed and dedicated in April 1881.

Reverend Nathaniel Hawthorne Gale organized a mission of the Methodist Episcopal Church (later the First Methodist Church) on April 18, 1880. An adobe building was built at the corner of Lead Avenue and Third Street late in 1881, and this became the first church in the New Town townsite. The previous year, Ashley and Gale had held services jointly in the courthouse before being turned out of those quarters. Once the Congregational Church was up, Ashley allowed the Methodists to share use of his building until they could get their own building. The current First Methodist Church, which was constructed in 1904 on the site of the original church, is in the National Register of Historic Places.

## New Town Public Library

423 Central Avenue NE
Albuquerque, NM 87102
505-848-1376

Growing Albuquerque wanted to be known as a progressive community. Establishment of a library lent credibility to the city's desire to attain some degree of cultural standing. Colonel Gordon Meylert got things started in the early 1880s when he saw to it that his swank San Felipe Hotel, located at Fifth Street and Gold Avenue, made space for a library room in lieu of a saloon. In the spring of 1891, a small group of socially prominent women led by Clara Fergusson (daughter of Franz Huning) and Mrs. William Hazeldine met in a parlor of the hotel and formulated plans for creating a free public library. Encouraged by editorials in the local press, they formed an association and commenced to solicit funds. In time, quarters were found in the Commercial Club at Fourth Street and Gold Avenue.

As the city grew, it became apparent that a private library association, dependent on funds from charity, would soon become inadequate for the task of providing literature to the citizens. It was obvious that the municipality must assume responsibility for a library system. The impetus for that move came from Joshua and Sarah Raynolds, who were owners of Perkins Hall

Special Collections Library. *Historic Albuquerque Inc., Nancy Tucker Collection.*

at Railroad and Edith and part owners of the First National Bank of Albuquerque. Perkins Hall had briefly housed the Albuquerque Academy in 1890–92 and later the Albuquerque High School.

In 1900, the Raynoldses agreed to deed Perkins Hall and four adjacent lots to the city for use as a new public library. The gift, coinciding with the merger of the private library association and a newly established municipal library board, marked the authentic beginning of the Albuquerque Public Library. The new library opened on May 1, 1901. The library home remained at Perkins Hall until 1923, when a small fire damaged the structure. Believing that repairs would be too costly, the city commission demolished the building the following year and put up a new library in 1925 (which still stands) in the by then fashionable Pueblo-Spanish architectural style.

The first public library building is now the Special Collections Library.

# INFRASTRUCTURE DEVELOPMENTS IN NEW TOWN

**F**ires that devasted entire cities were an acknowledged fact of life in nineteenth-century America. The people of Albuquerque recognized the threat and organized a volunteer fire company soon after the railroad came.

Roads and streets were constructed as the city grew. Horses and buggies and bicycles needed smooth surfaces to transport people among New Town, Old Town and the railroad yards to the south of New Town. And then came the automobile. J.L. Dodson, a local bicycle dealer, gets credit for introducing the motor car to the city. It was a small buggy with wire-spoke wheels and a small gas engine. Dodson went to Denver in November 1897 to collect his purchase and began a drive home that would take five days. People in horse and buggies were in danger when horses saw the automobile because they panicked and ran off. Gasoline had to be sent in by railroad and picked up at towns along the way. Yet in spite of all, Mr. Dodson and his automobile prevailed and reached Albuquerque safely. This automobile was the only automobile in the city for two years.

Automobiles competed with buggies for many years on roads designed for buggies. It wasn't until the 1920s that automobile travel across the state took off and interstate travel needs became more important.

Downtown flooding was always a threat. The site of New Town, lower than Old Town by several feet, was known to be vulnerable to floodwaters. The fact that the old river channel went between Alameda and Barelas through the region just west of the tracks was a reminder that the 1874 flood could happen again.

Progressive thinkers in early New Town recognized that the residents should be proactive in addressing flood threats. The issue was bigger than the townsite, and they enlisted personnel in the county. They were successful, as in 1883 Bernalillo County formed a River Commission, with power to levy a small assessment of all property within five miles of the Rio Grande. The money thereby derived was earmarked for the construction of earthworks at points where the river was prone to break through its banks.

Just a year later, the town got a real threat of flooding. The mountains to the north had received an enormous snowpack. Flooding was expected. Angus Grant, Santiago Baca, civil engineer W.F. Hill and other civic leaders undertook a tour of the river in the Alameda region, where the river had made its turn to the west centuries earlier. They wanted to look over the river and assess the state of precautionary measures that could be taken to prevent overflow into the lowlands caused by the presence of the earlier Rio Grande channel. They felt that the most vulnerable place was about two miles north of Alameda and suggested building a dike at that point. Such a dike should contain the swollen river and prevent floodwaters from returning to the old channel that ran through New Albuquerque. Workers were enlisted and a lengthy dike was constructed. When the floodwaters came, workers traveled to the dike and surrounding region to ensure that the river control was maintained. The new dike had some weaknesses that were addressed by emergency crews, but it held under flows that were the highest recorded. New Albuquerque had been saved by good preparations and an emergency squad that had labored under extreme conditions.

Periodic flooding was a constant threat to New Albuquerque, and residents recognized that more needed to be done. Soon after the flood threat of 1884 had subsided, residents gathered to ask Congress for an appropriation to fund flood control. Specifically, they wanted a series of levees built along the riverbank to provide security for both Old and New Town. This turned out to be a lengthy process.

In anticipation of a long process to get federal funds, residents of the city and county took immediate action. They initiated construction of levees, installed riprap where the river was prone to bank-cutting, dug drainage ditches and reinforced bridges. In 1891, through the joint efforts of the city and county, a larger and more substantial dike was completed at Alameda to replace the original 1884 structure. Rows of willows were planted in front of the new barrier to serve as a breakwater, and the earthworks were seeded in hope that grass cover would forestall erosion.

Some mitigation of floodwaters from the mesas on the east occurred. Eight arroyos drained the Sandia Mountains, and drainage from these channels, covering an eighty- to one-hundred-square-mile region, presented a hazard. The new railroad tracks had borrow ditches on either side, and when cloudbursts occurred, they became small rivers. The tracks caught the full force of the runoff, and bridges spanning the lateral arroyos caught the forces of these sudden floods.

The flooding problem in the Middle Valley was finally addressed with the organization of the Middle Rio Grande Conservancy District (MRGCD) in 1925. The district was formed to control floods in the Albuquerque Basin and manage the irrigation systems. The conservancy was responsible for the stretch of river from Cochiti Pueblo to the north to the Elephant Butte Reservoir in the south. Levees, drainage ditches and dams in the headwaters of the Rio Grande became major factors in addressing the flooding problems in the New Town region.

During the growth of Albuquerque into the surrounding mesas, heavy summer rain falling on the mesas collected in the arroyos and discharged through the valley area of Albuquerque into the Rio Grande. Downtown Albuquerque was seriously affected. The city was expanding into the mesas, land development removed natural vegetation and the construction of rooftops, streets and parking lots increased the amount of runoff that went into the valley from both directions. This problem was addressed with the development of the Albuquerque Metropolitan Arroyo Flood Control Authority (AMAFCA). The MRGCD and AMAFCA are discussed in more detail later in this chapter.

## First Fire Station in New Town
Original Station Located at First Street and Gold Avenue SW

In the beginning, the New Mexico Town Company had no equipment, and firemen had to rely on bucket brigades to combat fires. The principal source of water was the Lower Barelas Canal, which crossed Railroad Avenue between Second and Third Streets. Its flow was not always reliable, and to make matters worse, residents commonly befouled the waters with sewage.

In 1882, through efforts related to the board of trade, enough contributions were raised to purchase the town's first fire cart. Sheriff Perfecto Armijo, another son of Ambrosio, and several businessmen donated materials for a

Early fire engine in 1901. *Historic Albuquerque Inc., Walter Haussamen Collection.*

station, a small wooden building erected on First Street near Gold Avenue. This became the city's first fire station.

With the creation of a formal town government in 1885, additional equipment was authorized and purchased by the board of trustees and a new, larger station was rented on Railroad Avenue. Also, the board designated a formal fire zone whose north–south boundaries were between the tracks and Fifth Street, with the east–west boundaries between Copper and Lead Avenues. Ordinances prohibited further construction of frame buildings and storage of oil, gunpowder and other flammable materials inside the zone.

There were three volunteer companies that had fire carts. Even with these efforts, three fires consumed major buildings at the end of the nineteenth century: the Armijo House in 1897, the Grant Opera House building in 1898 and the San Felipe Hotel in 1899.

## Telephone Museum of New Mexico

110 Fourth Street NW
Albuquerque, NM 87102
505-842-2937

The telephone came to New Town in 1882. It was reported that there were fifty subscribers. The service was started by Miguel Otero Sr. The

AT&T Telephone Museum. *Roger Zimmerman Collection.*

location was in the 100 block of Railroad Avenue. The telephone was not immediately popular, and the total number of subscribers was just thirty-four in 1883. In 1886, the Colorado Telephone Company bought out Otero. A competing Mutual Automatic Telephone Company was organized in 1901. The Colorado Telephone System bought out the Mutual Automatic Company in 1906. There was no long-distance service until 1911.

The Telephone Museum of New Mexico is housed in a building built in 1906 for the telephone company. The museum includes three floors of communication equipment in unique exhibits. The museum features historical displays, photographs and literature from the early days of the telephone industry. The Telephone Museum is open from 10:00 a.m. to 2:00 p.m. Mondays, Wednesdays and Fridays.

## McCanna/Hubbell Building

424 Central Avenue SW
Albuquerque, NM 87102

Privately owned utilities were soon providing New Town residents with a number of the amenities that residents of more cosmopolitan areas had come to expect. Perfecto Armijo, businessman and occasional sheriff, secured

Nighttime picture of exterior of Albuquerque Gas & Electric Building, circa 1930. *Albuquerque Museum, 1978.151.024, Brooks Studio Collection.*

the city's first electric franchise in 1882. Perfecto, Dennis Dennison and Angus A. Grant formed the Albuquerque Electric Company. Armijo sold his interest in the company, and Dennison became president. The company installed lights in some of the streets and public buildings in 1883. It was then known as the Albuquerque Electric Light Company. The company reorganized in 1886 as the Electric Light Company of Albuquerque and elected Angus Grant as the president.

The Albuquerque Gas Company, whose initial board listed Huning as president and Hazeldine as secretary, erected a plant in 1882 that took coal, bought in by the railway, and converted it to gas in 1882. Initially, the gas was used for illumination of the streets, but it eventually spread into nearby buildings. Gaslights proved not only a decided convenience but also helped to check crime in the dance hall district that had sprouted near the tracks. Bryan reported that Albuquerque saloonkeeper W.E. Talbott traded in his gaslights for incandescent electric lamps in 1883.

Angus Grant was a construction contractor for the AT&SF railroad. He took up residence in Albuquerque in 1880 and quickly got into the utilities business. He got into the water distribution business as well as gas and electricity. When he died in 1901, he was considered as the largest individual property owner in Albuquerque, having holdings in the water, gas and electric light plants.

In 1902, the gas and electric companies were merged into the Albuquerque Gas, Electric Light and Power Company (AGELPC). The AGELPC was located at the corner of Railroad and Broadway until 1905. There were two moves before it settled in the McCanna/Hubbell Building in 1915. AGELPC became Public Service Company of New Mexico (PNM) in 1946 and remained in that location until 1968.

## Barelas Bridge
Original Bridges located West of Bridge Boulevard and Fourth Street SW

The passage of the Rio Grande through central New Mexico has been a challenge to development by humans. In the Albuquerque region, it was said that the Rio Grande could be one hundred yards wide during low flow and up to a mile wide during severe flooding. With the coming of the railroad, Albuquerque was growing in importance as a commercial center for New Mexico, and it became important to improve transportation opportunities to the farm and pasture lands west of the river. One good area for agriculture was Atrisco. People in Atrisco wanted to go to market or church in Old Town. When the river was low, the citizens could roll up their trousers or skirts and wade across. At other times, they might have to resort to log canoes or skiffs, which they propelled with long poles. In 1856, a ferryboat was built for crossings near the Barelas ford. The ferry was a low, narrow barge, and two to four large men would propel it. For more than two decades, the ferry hauled people, livestock, stagecoaches and freight wagons over the river's muddy waters.

This lack of a good crossing of the Rio Grande was an unsatisfactory situation to the New Town developers, and they created the Albuquerque Bridge Company in 1879. Elias Stover served as president, Franz Huning as vice-president and William Hazeldine as secretary. They sold stock and got a bridge underway in 1881. A timber bridge was opened to the public on December 12, 1882. The river span was six hundred feet, and the approach on marshy bottomland added another five hundred feet. A tollhouse in the center collected five cents per person. Horsemen were required to walk their mounts.

Barelas Bridge, circa 1910. *Albuquerque Museum, 1973.012.011, Diane Gerow Collection.*

The bridge proved to be a financial disaster. When the river was low, people waded across the river to avoid paying the toll. When the river was high, it usually damaged part of the structure and the company had high repair costs. A particularly destructive flood damaged the bridge beyond repair in May 1891, and the company went out of business. Franz Huning, as principal investor, lost thousands in the venture

Groups in New Town continued to pursue keeping a bridge open at the Barelas crossing. During this period, most of the bridges in the territory were of simple, timber-beam construction that were not designed by engineers. It isn't clear when the county became more involved, but in 1903, the New Mexico Territory approved the Territorial Road Act of 1903, which provided funding and engineering assistance for New Mexico counties. Now counties would get help and oversight from the territorial government.

In 1909, the New Mexico Good Roads Association was formed. During the first year of the commission, the Barelas steel truss bridge over the Rio Grande was approved and built. This was a high-quality bridge designed to remain in place during the flood season. Thus, Albuquerque had good transportation capabilities to a satellite neighborhood.

## Initial Water Supply in Old Town

Before 1875, citizens would go to the river and collect water in barrels. They would let the mud and particles in the water settle in the barrels and then would skim off the clear fluid at the top. Elias Stover is credited with getting the first water system going. Because of the high water table, he sank a pipe in the center of town on the plaza. He and his partner, Crary, owned a store and placed the pipe in front of it. Clear water would be easily retrieved with a hand pump. A tin was available for priming, and anyone who brought their own bucket was welcome to all that they wanted.

## Initial Water Supply in New Town

As New Town developed, there was a limited need for a centralized water supply system. Hotels and larger establishments had water supplies as early as 1883, but most residents found it simpler and cheaper to sink a shallow well in their own backyards. According the city historical records, a city reservoir was established near Yale and Redondo with a nearby well in about 1886. In 1891, the city had two wells near the water works pumping facility at the corner of Broadway and Tijeras Avenue. The waterworks wells and facility were expanded at this location, and by 1902, there were 109 fire hydrants in existence.

## Middle Rio Grande Conservancy District

1931 Second Street SW
Albuquerque, NM 87102
505-247-0234 | https://www.mrgcd.com

The formation of the MRGCD in 1925 gave Albuquerque citizens the comfort that the flooding threat was finally going to be addressed. The MRGCD created a plan in 1927 to address flood protection and channel improvement over the length of the project. This initial part of the plan was to construct levees spaced from 1,500 to 2,000 feet apart that would outline the Rio Grande. Within this span, there would be an inner-flow channel that was 600 to 750 feet in width. The function of the wide channel would be to pass the high floods, which may occur in intervals of

MRGCD levees and drainage ditches to control the Rio Grande. *Courtesy of Middle Rio Grande Conservancy District.*

fifteen to twenty years and prevent overflow to adjacent lands. The inner low-flow channel would carry the annual floods and would be expected to help with silt buildup.

Higher levees were placed in Albuquerque as additional protection from floods. Drainage ditches would be located next to the levees. The material removed from those ditches would provide fill for the levees that were eight to ten feet above the low water elevation of the river. The levee and ditch would have a minimum berm of twenty feet to keep the functions separate. Mechanisms would be instituted to protect the levees from scour. The drainage ditches would help reduce the elevation of the high ground water table. Levees and drainage ditches can easily be seen at any of bridges crossing the Rio Grande.

The MRGCD recognized the need to use dams to temporarily store floodwaters so that they could be released in subpeak flows. They worked in conjunction with the U.S. Bureau of Reclamation to build the El Vado Storage Dam in 1935. Cochiti, Angostura, Isleta and San Acacia diversion dams were constructed to channel water into irrigation canals for each section of the river. Even then, while a master plan for drainage and flood control had been devised, it took decades before the massive sums of money became available for the remaining needed work. As late as 1941, a segment of the levees gave way, funneling a mighty stream of water down First Street and causing $1 million worth of damage.

The developments of the vast federal installations at Kirtland Air Force Base prompted the U.S. government to tackle the potential flood problem on a grand scale. In 1950, the Army Corps of Engineers initiated work on the Jemez Canyon dam to check flash floods on the Jemez River. That was followed by construction of Abiquiu Dam on another tributary of the Rio Grande, the Rio Chama. Finally, in the late 1970s, the huge Cochiti Dam was completed on the Rio Grande itself. These structures not only permitted the impounding and controlled release of floodwaters but also held back the silt that otherwise would be carried to the Middle Valley and deposited in the main channel, thereby decreasing chances of the river leaving its banks during the spring and summer runoffs.

The second major responsibility of the MRGCD was to manage the irrigation systems. Irrigation practices had significant roots in the past. The Pueblo people of the Rio Grande had developed primitive irrigation systems in the valley by the tenth century. These systems used a main *acequia* (shared irrigation ditch) into which water was diverted from the river, and then it was directed along *acequias* and distributed laterally with secondary ditches to specified properties. Maintenance of the main *acequia* would be a community responsibility.

In most areas, the goal was to reduce the water table in the New Town region by four to six feet. This was accomplished by the active construction of MRGCD drainage ditches and the effects of well pumping associated with residential and industrial development in the downtown area.

## Flood Control Authority

2600 Prospect Avenue NE
Albuquerque, NM 87107
505-884-2215 | http://amafca.org

A series of floods in the early 1950s caused considerable damage in the east mesa heights and valley areas, and the Army Corps of Engineers was asked to make a study of the problem. The Corps proposed construction

AMAFCA north drainage ditch. *Roland Penttila, photographer.*

of two diversion channels on the east mesa, one going north and the other south. Construction of these channels would divert floodwaters from the Middle Valley area. In 1955, Congress authorized federal funds for the construction of these diversion channels provided that a local government would assume certain responsibilities. These responsibilities were payment of part of the construction cost, purchase of channel right-of-way, construction of highway bridges and relocation of utility lines. This was accomplished in what was to become the Albuquerque Metropolitan Arroyo Flood Control Authority (AMAFCA).

AMAFCA is a local government subdivision created in 1963 to protect persons and property from flash floods in regions above the downtown floodplain. The district included the city of Albuquerque and neighboring areas in Bernalillo County. The authority collects property taxes to construct and maintain flood control facilities.

Floodwaters from the east mesa are channeled into an elaborate and extensive set of drains that feed the two diversion channels. The North Diversion Channel started at Campus wash near the university and was constructed northward along the edge of the mesa until it got near the Alameda neighborhood. The channel then emptied into the Alameda Outlet Structure, which carried the water into the Rio Grande. Bridges for highways and the railroad had to be built. This diversion channel is counterintuitive, as the channel flows to the north while the Rio Grande flows to the south. The mesa is sufficiently higher than the downtown area so that the diversion channel grade dropping northward could be adequately constructed.

The South Diversion Channel started near Central Avenue, and the I-25 freeway and was directed south, where it emptied into Tijeras Canyon. Bridges for highways and one under the railroad were needed as well.

# PRIVATE AND PUBLIC EDUCATION DEVELOPMENTS IN NEW TOWN

The education of youth is always recognized as an important part of any community development. Until the railroad came, education was largely handled by the Catholic Church in Old Town. The residents were primarily Hispanos who were involved in working the land, participating in church activities and defending themselves from neighboring raiders. There was not a major emphasis on gaining an education for the working class, but the wealthy landowners and traders did value education. Many of the Armijo clan went to college in Missouri.

The Catholic Church initiated activities to improve the education of a growing population in the Middle Valley. In 1851, Bishop Jean-Baptiste Lamy enticed several religious orders—the Sisters of Loretto, the Christian Brothers and the Sisters of Charity—to send him teachers to staff the English schools he was busily setting up. The church recognized the need for Hispanos to learn to function in an American society. This request was further amplified when the Jesuits took charge of Albuquerque's San Felipe de Neri Church in 1868. The Jesuit Order has a responsibility to educate youth. In 1872, the Jesuits managed to open a school for sixty boys in quarters rented from County Commissioner Ambrosio Armijo. The school received some income from the territorial legislature to assist in this educational mission since there were no public schools. An issue that developed was whether nuns could wear habits when teaching in public-assisted schools.

The developments of education in private schools appeared to stimulate the territorial legislature to address the needs for public education. There was a need to provide education for students who didn't require family financial support. In 1891, the territorial legislature accepted its responsibility to provide public education, and the Albuquerque Public School System was organized on February 12, 1891. The new law authorized municipalities to establish school boards and sell municipal bonds for school construction. Schools for all grades were constructed, with elementary schools being located in each of the four wards. It is recalled that Colonel Marmon laid out the Albuquerque townsite and divided it into quadrants, called wards. The elementary schools offered grades one to six.

A new Central School, which was located at Third Street and Lead, was opened for the upper grades in 1900. It was the high school before Albuquerque High School was built. This building is still in existence. For the preceding seven years, secondary school students had studied in a building on south Edith. Several buildings were used to house the students in the higher grades until Albuquerque's first high school was built in 1914. In 1914, newly constructed Albuquerque High School acquired a permanent campus on the corner of Broadway and Central. This building still exists and now contains nice condominiums conveniently located for the downtown area. Albuquerque did not acquire another high school until 1948, when Highland High was constructed in the East Heights.

There are two people who made major contributions to getting the University of New Mexico located near New Town: Bernard S. Rodey and Colonel Gordon W. Meylert. Rodey was a thirty-two-year-old lawyer who was a Bernalillo County senator in the territorial legislature. He was the champion of the project. Part of the feature of the bill was that land would be available for the university and its growth. Colonel Meylert bought more than twenty acres of land on the east mesa. The high and dry land was within two miles of the railroad and was well outside the limits of New Town, which meant that it had room to grow. Meylert, owner of the San Felipe Hotel, donated the land to the Territory of New Mexico for use as a university site. This contribution went far to ensure that Albuquerque got the university.

Rodey took a rough bill, prepared by another attorney, and drafted it into a legislative bill that he could introduce. The bill was presented near the end of the legislative session in 1889. Other legislators, like the one from Las Cruces, were thinking along the same lines, but they wanted the state university to be in their hometowns. Rodey and the champions of the bill wisely proposed that other institutions with different functions should be placed in these competing towns and that the state would benefit from diversity of education and function. This is how Albuquerque got the

Albuquerque High School in 1915. *Historic Albuquerque Inc., Nancy Tucker Collection.*

university, Socorro got the School of Mines, Las Cruces got the Land Grant College of Agriculture and Mechanical Arts and Las Vegas got the Insane Asylum. Santa Fe had already captured the state penitentiary in 1885, so it was not included in the bill.

Rodey's bill, supported by a coalition of progressive forces, succeeded in overcoming the opposition and won passage on February 28, 1889, in the waning hours of the session. Rodey's bill was signed into law by Governor Edmund G. Ross early in 1889. His successor, Governor L. Bradford Prince, appointed the university's first board of regents on September 2, 1889. Members included Mariano S. Otero of Bernalillo, Gordon W. Meylert as secretary/treasurer and Elias S. Stover as the university's first president. The new board of regents worked to get the university organized, faculty hired, students enrolled and buildings constructed to handle the load. The first building for the university was Hodgin Hall, which will be discussed later.

## St. Vincent Academy for Girls
Initial Location at Sixth Street and Lomas Avenue NW

In 1880, the Catholic Church took steps to improve educational offerings. There weren't many students involved in the church-based education program. Father Gasparri, rector of San Felipe de Neri Parish, invited the Sisters of Charity from Santa Fe to come to Old Albuquerque and take over the church's education program. His request, in part, allowed the Jesuit priests to concentrate their attentions on regular ecclesiastical duties in the expanding San Felipe de Neri Parish that was fueled by the railroad construction. The nuns agreed with the provision that a convent be constructed to house them and provide facilities for teaching. With unexpected help from Sister Blandina Segale, a native of Genoa, Italy, this was accomplished.

By September 1881, even with construction of the convent not complete, the Sisters were ready for the fall term. Initially, they used temporary facilities and eventually opened two school rooms in their convent: the Parochial Our Lady of the Angels Private School for girls and the separate Old Town Public School for boys and girls. Nuns taught in the private school and the Jesuit fathers in the public school.

With the significant changes to the Middle Valley due to the coming of the railroad, Sister Blandina and the Sisters of Charity soon expanded their horizons and decided to invest in the mushrooming growth of New Albuquerque. They secured sixty-four lots in this new townsite, cornering on Sixth and New York Avenue (later Lomas). In 1882, the nuns initiated work on a new private school, which was completed and opened as a public day school. The St. Vincent Academy for girls for grades 1–12 functioned from 1884 to 1969.

## Albuquerque Academy
Last Location at Railroad Avenue and Edith Boulevard NE

Another private school emerged with the coming of the railroad, this one with a Protestant sponsor. In 1879, a representative of Colorado College of Colorado Springs appeared in Old Town with a proposal. His institution was promoting the establishment of private academies in the western territories, where public school systems had not yet come into being. He was looking for support from some of Albuquerque's wealthy and influential citizens to organize an academy. With support from the community, he would provide teachers and guarantee their salaries under the name of the Albuquerque Academy. The offer was readily accepted.

The original Albuquerque Academy was incorporated under the laws of the territory, and it received its first pupils on October 14, 1879. The academy was the only school in the area offering a complete curriculum for grades 1–12. The board of trustees for the school included Elias S. Stover, William Hazeldine, Franz Huning and Adolph Harsch, owner of the Coyote Bottling Works.

In 1879, the school occupied a small adobe building northeast of the plaza in Old Town and had twenty-six students. Professor Charles W. Howe of Colorado College served as the first principal, and he had two assistants. The academy grew rapidly and flourished, and the trustees transferred the main campus to New Albuquerque in 1881, although a branch continued to be maintained in Old Town. Another branch was operated on Arno Street in the Highlands. By 1890, with enrollment having expanded to 385, the Academy consolidated and moved into a new three-story building, called Perkins Hall, which was located at the corner of Railroad Avenue and Edith Boulevard.

After the public school legislation in 1891, it appears that the city residents were ready for public education and that the Albuquerque Academy was not needed. The city essentially took over the upper-level Albuquerque Academy students, who became part of Albuquerque High School. The city rented Perkins Hall to house the new Albuquerque High School and hired the Albuquerque Academy's last principal, Charles E. Hodgin, to be the first public school superintendent.

Note that Albuquerque has a highly regarded Albuquerque Academy that was started as a boys' school for grades 6–12 in 1955. It is now a highly rated independent coeducational college preparatory school. The new academy has no ties to the earlier academy.

## St. Mary's School
224 Seventh Street NW
Albuquerque, NM 87102
505-242-6271

The emergence of the public schools in Albuquerque stimulated interests by the Jesuits in starting a school in New Town. In 1892, they opened a school, the Immaculate Conception School, in rented quarters on the southeast corner of Sixth and Railroad (Central). The institution has since been known as St. Mary's. At first, it accepted only boys, while girls attended nearby St. Vincent's Academy. For many years, St. Mary's had grades 1–12, but now the school offers grades 1–8.

## Hodgin Hall at UNM

1889 Central Avenue NE
Albuquerque, NM 87106
505-277-5808

By 1892, a three-story gabled structure of red brick had been built as the first building at the University of New Mexico. The building was in the Richardsonian Romanesque style, a contemporary variant of Victorian architecture, to somewhat emulate similar buildings at other institutions of higher learning. It is apparent that the originators wanted the facility to have the traditional academic look found in schools farther east.

Originally, the first building was called the Main Building and then the Administration Building; finally, in 1936, it was named for Charles E. Hodgin, a member of the university's first graduating class in 1894. Mr. Hodgin was the first superintendent of the Albuquerque Public Schools and then joined UNM to be a distinguished professor and administrator at the university. Hodgin Hall is located on the university campus and is in the National Register of Historic Places. It houses the UNM Alumni Association.

Structural problems with the building's roof gave university president William Tight the opportunity to remodel the building in 1908. He chose to

Hodgin Hall at University of New Mexico, circa 1902. *Albuquerque Museum, 1978.050.701, courtesy of University of New Mexico.*

have the building remodeled in the Pueblo Revival style that complemented construction of a new boiler plant, two dormitories and a fraternity meeting house in previous years. This was a major change to the university's architectural thinking and became the model for future university buildings.

## United States Indian Training School
Original Location at Twelfth Street and 101 Indian School Road NW
Albuquerque, NM

For some years before 1880, the U.S. government had expressed an interest in opening an industrial school for Native Americans somewhere in Central New Mexico. Presbyterian missionaries had learned of the planned institution and expressed an interest in establishing and operating it. The government at that time was in the habit of contracting with various Protestant denominations to run these so-called Indian schools. Reverend Sheldon Jackson, regional head of the Presbyterial Board of Home Missions, submitted a proposal to the secretary of the interior to establish an Indian school in Albuquerque and manage it until the federal authorities were prepared to assume full charge. His plan won approval.

On January 1, 1881, the United States Indian Training School, commonly known as the Albuquerque Indian School, opened in rented quarters a mile north of the Old Town Plaza. The first class of about forty pupils was composed mainly of Pueblos, Apaches and Utes. The youngsters, who boarded at the school, were taught a variety of academic and vocational subjects, designed mainly to hasten their integration into American economic and social systems. The curriculum was modeled after that of the celebrated Indian Industrial School at Carlisle, Pennsylvania. Both the government and the Presbyterians were motivated by a keen desire to see the Native American youth transformed into upstanding American citizens.

Albuquerque businessmen, eager to see the new institution find a permanent home, raised $500 and purchased a sixty-six-acre farm north of Old Town, which they donated to the Department of the Interior. In the fall of 1882, the school moved to the new campus at the corner of Twelfth Street and Indian School Road. Since agriculture was one of the vocational subjects taught to male students, they worked a part of each weekday in the fields, producing most of the food needed for the school's tables. Boys also received instruction in such crafts as carpentry and stonecutting, while girls studied cooking, sewing and care of the sick.

In October 1886, the Presbyterians voluntarily withdrew from management of the school, and the U.S. government took control. It grew and improved to become a recognized educational facility for Native Americans in the West. It closed in the 1980s due to changing priorities among the Native American populations. The Albuquerque school structures eventually fell victim to fire and deterioration and were razed in 1985. The school property was transferred to the All Indian Pueblo Council, and now the site houses buildings that can be used for special Indian programs such as training.

## Menaul School
301 Menaul Boulevard NE
Albuquerque, NM 87107
505-347-7727 | http://www.menaulschool.org

Although the Presbyterians relinquished control over the Indian school, their interest in Native American education at Albuquerque remained strong. In 1886, the church acquired a two-hundred-acre tract just below the sand hills north of downtown Albuquerque and launched the Presbyterial Industrial School, a mission trade school for Native Americans. Within months, they raised a four-story brick building and three frame structures to provide evidence that a campus was in place. Unfortunately, a disastrous fire practically destroyed the school in 1887. The effects of the fire and competition from the federal Indian school, expanding at an accelerating rate a short distance to the west, proved to be problems so significant that the Presbyterian Home Mission Board elected to close its mission school in 1891.

The Presbyterians found a new mission in education: to educate Hispanos. In 1896, Reverend James A. Menaul, a Presbyterian minister, sought and received Presbyterian mission funding for a boarding school that would serve Spanish-speaking boys from New Mexico, primarily from the northern portion of the state. The school would serve educational needs in regions where public education was practically nonexistent. It was not unusual for parents to contribute to their children's education with contributions of grain or livestock. They used the two hundred acres that had originally been purchased for the private Indian school.

The original Indian school facility was reopened with a new orientation and purpose in Albuquerque in 1896. This new school took the name

Menaul School. *Historic Albuquerque Inc., Nancy Tucker Collection.*

Menaul Training School to honor the memory of Reverend James A. Menaul, who had served sixteen years as a missionary in the territory and established Albuquerque's First Presbyterian Church. The school is in the National Register of Historic Places.

The school is still functioning and occupies a prominent place among New Mexico's private (and now coeducational) institutions.

# REALIGNMENT OF ROUTE 66

Route 66 was one of the federal highways that crossed the state that was heavily involved in both the migration of people during the 1930s and in expanding the horizons of interstate travelers who were introduced to different cultures and ethnic groups in the arid Southwest. US 66 became bigger than life and still commands a nostalgia enjoyed by travelers from all over the world. It has become the most famous highway in the United States. Memories transcend the travel experience to bring about a state of excitement. Almost anything connected with Route 66 exhibits that kind of magic. Albuquerque was in the middle of many significant developments on Route 66.

The federal government had a prominent role in the development of Route 66. The American Association of State Highway Transportation Officials (AASHTO) went through phases in initiating and implementing the federal highway system. Routes were established and numbered in December 1925, and then there were modifications as the reality of the situation became apparent in many of the states. Finally, in August 1926, the final designations were made. US 66 was to be an east–west highway that went from Chicago to Los Angeles through an alignment in New Mexico that went from Tucumcari in the east to Gallup in the west. The original US 66 route in 1926 went from Santa Rosa to Romeroville (near Las Vegas) through Santa Fe to Bernalillo, Albuquerque and Los Lunas and then to Laguna, Grants and Gallup. These were existing roadways that served local intrastate transportation needs.

A.T. Hannett was the governor when US 66 was designated by the federal government. He had been on the state highway commission from 1923 to 1924 and knew of the planned implementation of the federal highway system in New Mexico. He was aware that 107 miles of travel over unpaved roads could be saved by interstate travelers if the road were shortened between Santa Rosa and Laguna. This shortening would cause major cities, including Santa Fe, to be removed from the revenues of interstate travel. He had a supporter in Clyde Tingley, who was the ex-officio mayor of Albuquerque and was also working as a district maintenance supervisor for the state highway department. Both of these individuals were Democrats. Hannett was running for reelection in 1926 against Richard C. Dillon, who was a Republican and was against the Route 66 shortening. Dillon was catering to northern voters, like ones in Santa Fe, and had declared that he would not support building a shortcut between Santa Rosa and Albuquerque, which would reduce the US 66 travel distance by 90 miles.

The election was held on November 6, 1926, and Governor Hannett lost. He decided that he would construct the Santa Rosa cut-off between Santa Rosa and Moriarty, a distance of sixty-nine miles, of which twenty-seven miles didn't have any roads at all, before he left office. Incoming governor Dillon said that he would stop construction of any shortcut that was not functioning when he took office. This set the stage for a major construction effort. Late in November, Governor Hannett authorized the highway department to construct the cut-off and have it completed before January 1, 1927.

Governor Hannett borrowed some funds from other state accounts and authorized district highway engineer E.B. Bail to construct the shortcut. Bail got two individuals to be project leaders, one starting at Santa Rosa going west and the other at Moriarty going east, and they were to work as hard as they could to complete the project. The new highway, called NM 6, would go from Santa Rosa to Moriarty, and then travelers could follow the new US 470 from Moriarty to Albuquerque, where the original US 66 could be picked up again.

Holidays for Thanksgiving, Christmas and the New Year were to be ignored by the work crews. Bail used a practice used in early New Mexico politics to stimulate the workers. It was standard procedure that a new governor would bring in his own workers for the highway department. Therefore, the existing workers were looking at being out of work come January 1. Bail challenged the workers to play a joke on the new governor. He is reported to have said something like, "Let's build this highway in spite of him and deliver it as accomplished. He couldn't withdraw a completed road."

The workers worked feverishly to accomplish the task in the thirty-one days that were eventually available. The weather was in the teens, it snowed during that month and the work was sometimes sabotaged by those who opposed the rerouting. But the workers had the road completed where cars could pass by January 3, 1927, which was the first time that the new governor could shut the project down. Governor Dillon accepted the *fait accompli* and, in a gesture of good will, did not fire the Hannett-appointed workers when he took office.

A main obstacle to constructing the accompanying Laguna cut-off to the west of Albuquerque was that two major rivers needed to be crossed: the Rio Grande and the Rio Puerco about nine miles farther west. Clyde Tingley knew that the Rio Grande was the most important because this bridge opened up travel to the west mesa and villages farther south and west. During the late 1920s, he worked to get the state highway department to construct an all-weather bridge across the Rio Grande on Central Avenue, and he succeeded. The bridge was completed in 1931.

With the accomplishment of the completion of the Central Avenue bridge, Clyde Tingley worked with the state highway commission to approve the Santa Rosa and Laguna cut-offs and recommend them to federal highway officials. This request was approved, and the federal government authorized federal funds to be spent on improvements of NM 6 between Santa Rosa and Laguna. Clyde Tingley became governor in 1935 and got to accept the official rerouting of US 66 in 1937.

## Unique Intersection: Central Avenue and Fourth Street NW

In 1926, US 66 was aligned along Fourth Street. In 1937, US 66 officially ran east–west through Albuquerque along Central Avenue and changed Albuquerque forever. The intersection of Central Avenue and Fourth Street in Albuquerque is a unique intersection that symbolizes the effects of establishing and changing federal highway alignments in New Mexico.

Clyde Tingley was instrumental in getting Albuquerque ready for US 66 realignment. With the Santa Rosa cut-off established through to the unique intersection, and being heavily used, the advantages of the shortcuts became evident. The possibility for all-weather traffic across the Rio Grande established the feasibility of having US 66 go directly west from Albuquerque.

Fourth Street and Central Avenue intersection. *Historic Albuquerque Inc., Diane Schaller Collection.*

After Clyde Tingley got the bridge built over the Rio Grande in 1931, the federal officials saw the benefit of the shorter route and funded construction of the new bridge across the Rio Puerco in 1933. Thus, the Laguna cut-off came to fruition, and a total of 107 miles of travel could be saved.

The impact on Albuquerque is that it changed from being a linear city to a cruciform, or cross-shaped, one. Growth occurred along Central Avenue as well as Fourth Street. The east mesa, which housed the university, became more populated. In 1938, Governor Clyde Tingley was successful in getting the state fair located on Central Avenue.

## US 85
Fourth Street NW and SW

Initially, US 85 and US 66 used Fourth Street to cross Albuquerque. US 85 went from Canada to El Paso, with an alignment in New Mexico from Raton in the north to Las Cruces in the south. US 85 was generally aligned with the Santa Fe Trail from the Colorado border to Santa Fe and then El

Camino Real south of Santa Fe to El Paso. El Camino Real was the principal north–south artery through the territory and later state. US 85 provided the federally funded roads to meet the needs of many citizens and visitors going in this direction. Fourth Street was used only for US 85 traffic after 1937.

## US 470/US 366
East of Fourth Street on Central Avenue NW

US 470 was a late addition in the final process of designating federal highways in New Mexico. Somehow between December 1925, when the federal highway system was announced, and August 1926, when the federal highway system was inaugurated, AASHTO succumbed to pressures from New Mexico to add a new highway, US 470. Part of the highway would be along the established road from the Estancia Valley to Santa Fe. This was an important route to support the farming activities in the Estancia Valley. The new federal highway went from Willard at the south to just north of Moriarty, and then it turned west toward Albuquerque. The intersection where US 470 made its turn to the west was the terminal point of the sixty-nine-mile Santa Rosa shortcut that was constructed by Hannett.

The road between Moriarty and Tijeras was essentially a wagon road and was seldom used in 1926, as it needed a lot of work. Once the travelers got over the Sedillo Hill going west, traffic between Tijeras and Albuquerque was well established. US 470 terminated at Fourth Street in Albuquerque.

US 470 was kind of an orphan to the U.S. highway system. From 1926 to 1931, it had the US 470 designation, and from 1931 to 1937, it was designated as US 366. It was eliminated entirely in 1937, and the north–south portion reverted back to a state highway, NM 41.

## Central Avenue Bridge
Central Avenue NW over the Rio Grande

It was known that the Rio Grande traveled through a heavily silted floodplain and that the channel was prone to shift its course during flooding. The sandy escarpment on the west side restricted easy movement to the west, while the flat floodplain to the east provided easy movement of raging waters. This situation challenged those who might want to establish a bridge across the river.

Central Bridge over Rio Grande in 1947. *Albuquerque Museum, 1982.181.128, courtesy of John Airy.*

Between 1927 and 1931, the New Mexico Highway Department worked feverishly to do things that would get the cut-offs accepted by the federal program and thus get US 66 rerouted. The city under ex-officio mayor Clyde Tingley arranged for state funds to build a bridge across the Rio Grande on Central Avenue to facilitate the Laguna cut-off. One of the arguments Clyde Tingley used was that Albuquerque needed a bridge to facilitate travel to the Albuquerque Airport on the west mesa. He was successful, and the bridge over the Rio Grande was completed in 1931.

Once the bridge over the Rio Puerco was completed, the shortcuts were brought up to federal highway standards by the time that the route was officially transferred from the longer north–south configuration to the shorter east–west alignment. The shorter version of Route 66 was officially accepted in October 1937. The subject of Hannett's joke and Tingley's dream had come to fruition.

## Railroad Underpass on Central Avenue
East of First Street on Central Avenue (Center of Address Quadrant)

There was a problem with bringing US 66 in from the east along the US 470 route. The new federal highway program required grade separations between highway traffic and railroads. Central Avenue crossed the AT&SF railroad, and this would be a problem with high-density interstate traffic. The realignment of US 66 was approved in 1931, with Clyde Tingley indicating that he would get nontransportation funds to construct an underpass for Central Avenue. He worked feverishly to get public works funds for the underpass and finally got support to construct the underpasses for both Central and Tijeras Avenues. They were completed in 1937.

Both underpasses are still in use. Both have required major drainage pathways to handle downtown flooding problems.

Central Avenue Underpass in 1936. *Albuquerque Museum, 1990.013.033.*

## El Vado Motel

2500 Central Avenue SW
Albuquerque, NM 87104
505-361-1667

Old properties on US 66 still have a special attraction to tourists. The El Vado Motel, built in 1937, has been refurbished as of 2018. Travelers can stay in original rooms and enjoy the ambiance of the glory days. It is interesting that *vado* in Spanish means "ford" in a river and that the motel is near the original ford in the Rio Grande. The El Vado Motel is listed in the National Register of Historic Places.

Perhaps the impact of US 66 on Albuquerque can be summarized by the following accounting of tourist courts in the city:

- three tourist courts on East Central in 1935, sixteen on Fourth Street
- thirty-seven tourist courts on Central in 1941
- ninety-eight tourist courts on Central in 1955

El Vado Motel, early Route 66 motel built in 1937. *Historic Albuquerque Inc., Jim Coad Collection.*

# COMMERCIAL AND GOVERNMENT AIRFIELDS

The first airfield in Albuquerque was constructed by Frank G. Speakman and William Langford Franklin in 1928. They were workers on the Santa Fe Railway and used grading equipment loaned by the city for after-hours work. They graded two runways on the east mesa, one approximately 5,300 feet long and the other just under 4,000 feet long. Gravity-fed fuel tanks were the only facilities associated with the runways. The venture was to become the Albuquerque Airport.

James G. Oxnard, a New York entrepreneur, bought out Franklin's share in the airport and renamed it Oxnard Field. He expanded the facility to 480 acres and added an administration building and other facilities. Oxnard Field continued as a private venture and served two competing airlines, Western Air Express and Transcontinental Air Transport, for about a year. The proximity of the Sandia Mountains to the east made pilots uneasy, and Western Air Express built a new facility, West Mesa Airport, across the Rio Grande in 1929.

The two competing airlines merged, forming Transcontinental and Western Air (TWA). Following the merger, all commercial air service shifted to the West Mesa Airport. This airport became known as Albuquerque Airport, while the original east mesa facility reverted to Oxnard Airport. The West Mesa Airport served Albuquerque until the competition of the new facility on the east mesa in 1939. It closed in 1967. West Mesa Airport was located on Airport Drive, which is a road going north from Central Avenue and west of Coors Boulevard. Traces of the runways have been removed.

In 1935, the city started to build a new public airport using Works Progress Administration (WPA) money. Mayor Clyde Tingley and the city leaders secured the funds for a construction of this civilian airport. The new Albuquerque Airport was four miles west of Oxnard Field on the same east mesa. Governor Clyde Tingley broke ground for the project on February 28, 1937. Albuquerque Municipal Airport opened in 1939 with two new paved runways, a Pueblo-style terminal building designed by Ernest Blumenthal and a massive hangar designed to accommodate the new Boeing 307 operated by TWA.

The merger between Western Air Express and Transcontinental Air Transport eventually became Trans World Airlines (TWA) in 1946. TWA merged with American Airlines in 2001. In essence, variations of TWA-scheduled flights were in and out of Albuquerque starting in 1929.

In January 1939, Major General Henry "Hap" Arnold, who became chief of the U.S. Army Air Corps, proposed to Congress that money be spent on a strong air defense. It soon became a national priority to secure airfields and bombing and gunnery ranges. An effort was also being made in cooperation with the WPA and Civil Aeronautics Authority to build up civilian airports of value to support national defense efforts.

Albuquerque city leaders began in 1939 to examine the possibility of adding an army air base to the east mesa and, through extensive negotiations with the U.S. Army Air Corps, succeeded in their efforts when the army established an air base that year. The Albuquerque Airport operations soon had a new role in 1940 when the civilian operations shared the new runways with the Albuquerque Army Air Base. The model was that the two operations would share use of the runways, but the army air base would handle rescue, firefighting and perimeter security operations. This arrangement, now with Kirtland Air Force Base, continues to this day. Don Alberts in his book, *Balloons to Bombers*, is credited with much of the information that follows.

## Old Commercial Air Terminal

2920 Yale Boulevard SE
Albuquerque, NM 87119
505-244-7700

The old terminal that was built in 1939 can be found just west of the Albuquerque International Sunport. The terminal served until 1965, when the present terminal was opened. It was the first commercial passenger

Old Albuquerque Terminal Building. *Historic Albuquerque Inc., Diane Schaller Collection.*

terminal in the state and is one of the few remaining historic transportation facilities left in the city.

TWA was the first airline using the terminal, and Continental Airlines was the second. Both started air service in Albuquerque in 1934 and used the terminal through their airlines' existence. Continental merged with United Air Lines in 2012. Other commercial traffic resumed after the war when Monarch Airlines came in 1947. Monarch became Frontier Airlines in 1950.

The building is still in use and hosts the Transportation Security Agency for Albuquerque. The building was used as the first location of the Albuquerque Museum, which was called the Museum of Albuquerque in 1967 when that city function was opened. The museum collection outgrew the available space at the terminal building, and a new building was built in Old Town in 1979. The air terminal building is in the National Register of Historic Places.

The Old Terminal offices in the building are being used, but the inside lobby is open to the public from 8:00 a.m. to 5:00 p.m. on weekdays. The interior is delightfully maintained to include high ceilings with herringbone latillas, rough-hewn beams, heavy wood columns with corbel brackets, rough-plastered walls, recessed bays with ornate wooden screens, tin chandeliers, flagstone floors and a corner fireplace.

## Sunport
2200 Sunport Boulevard SE
Albuquerque, NM 87119
505-244-7700

The east mesa commercial airport was renamed Albuquerque Sunport on April 17, 1963. The airport gained international status in 1971 and was renamed Albuquerque International Airport. The name was later changed to Albuquerque International Sunport in 1994, and this is the name used today.

## Albuquerque Army Air Base/Kirtland Field
2000 Wyoming Boulevard SE
Albuquerque, NM 87117
https://www.kirtland.af.mil

In support of a special arrangement with the city, the U.S. Army Air Corps leased two thousand acres neighboring and to the east of the Albuquerque Airport in 1941. Construction of Albuquerque Army Air Base began in January 1941 and was completed in August 1941. Albuquerque Army Air Base received its first military aircraft in March, and on April 1, 1941, a lone B-18 bomber landed on the north–south runway. With the assignment of five pilots to the aircraft, the day marked the official opening of Albuquerque Army Air Base.

The Albuquerque Army Air Base provided advanced flying training in primarily the B-17 Flying Fortress and the B-24 Liberator. The Nineteenth Bombardment Group arrived at Albuquerque Army Air Base in April 1941, shortly after the base was activated. The purpose was to train air and ground crews for reconnaissance and bombing duty on Boeing B-17s before deployment to Clark Field in the Philippines. The group focused on precision, high-altitude, and formation flying. They flew mock attacks on New Mexico villages and ranches under the command of Lieutenant Colonel Eugene Eubank (Eubank Boulevard was named for the colonel). The Nineteenth transferred to active duty in the Philippines in September 1941, a few months before the attack on Pearl Harbor on December 7.

The Nineteenth Bombardment Group was replaced by an Army Air Corps Ferrying Command School, which specialized in flying B-24 Liberator bombers. This command was responsible for ferrying bombers to Europe. The first contingent of trainees arrived on June 19, 1941. Using Link Trainers and B-24 training aircraft, TWA instructors trained more than 1,100 pilots and crewmen during the eight months that TWA operated the school.

In February 1942, the Albuquerque Army Air Base was named Kirtland Field in honor of Colonel Roy C. Kirtland, who was a prominent pioneer army pilot.

In addition to pilot training, Kirtland Field was tasked to provide bombardier training at its Advanced Flying School. The advanced bombardier school was started in December 1941, after Pearl Harbor. The first class of 61 bombardiers graduated on March 7, 1942, and by 1945, Albuquerque's bombardier's school had turned out 5,719 bombardiers and 1,750 regular pilots for the B-24 alone.

## Oxnard Field/Sandia Base

2000 Wyoming Boulevard SE
Albuquerque, NM 87117
https://www.kirtland.af.mil

In 1942, the army condemned 1,100 acres just east of Kirtland Field to form the Albuquerque Air Depot Training Station (informally called Sandia Base). This land included the hangars and runways at Oxnard Field. The purpose of the training station was to train aircraft mechanics and air depot service personnel. The old Oxnard Field hangars were used for training, and the runways were used to test-fly aircraft that had been repaired.

The air depot training continued until 1943, when that mission had been completed. At that time, the training station became the Albuquerque Army Air Field, which was separate from Kirtland Field. The airfield was relatively inactive until mid-1944, when military officials put the field to use to support the Army Air Forces Convalescent Center. Barracks and support facilities were used as quarters for about eight hundred wounded pilots and aircrewmen who were recovering from surgery and other medical services. This activity continued until April 1945.

At that time, the old army air field received another mission. The property became the demolition center for obsolete army aircraft. Aircraft were flown in, stripped of radio and fuel parts and the remaining structure was chopped into sections and melted into ingots. In the end, some 2,250 surplus military aircraft were disposed of.

Aerial photo of Kirtland (*foreground*) and Oxnard Fields (*background*) in 1945. *Courtesy of Sandia National Laboratories.*

In June 1945, the old army air field property on Oxnard Field was transferred to the army's Manhattan Engineer District in support of the Manhattan Project, and in September of that year, it officially became known as Sandia Base. The air field had no future flight mission. The runways were removed, and buildings were built on the remaining mesa property.

The U.S. Atomic Energy Act of 1946 established the Atomic Energy Commission (AEC) as the civilian agency that would control the development and production of nuclear weapons. The AEC succeeded the Manhattan Engineer District on January 1, 1947, in taking care of the nation's nuclear program.

There was a separation of responsibilities between the civilian and military programs. The Armed Forces Special Weapons Project (AFSWP) became the military agency responsible for aspects of nuclear weapons remaining under military control. These responsibilities included maintenance, storage, surveillance, security, handling of nuclear weapons and supporting nuclear testing activities. The AFSWP was staffed by army, navy and soon-to-be-formed air force personnel.

In 1947, Z-Division of Los Alamos Laboratory was a civilian organization located in Albuquerque to support AEC functions. AFSWP created an organization to support those activities. The next chapter discusses how Sandia Base and Kirtland Field joined Manzano Base to become Kirtland Air Force Base.

# MANHATTAN PROJECT AND KIRTLAND AIR FORCE BASE

The United States found need to develop an atomic weapon as a means to end World War II. The Manhattan Project was a code name for the secret, America-led effort to develop a functional atomic weapon. The name "Manhattan" comes from the Army Corps of Engineers District in New York City. The project was headed by Major General Leslie Groves, who had headed the project to build the Pentagon, and he was put in charge of the Manhattan Project in September 1942. He participated in selection of sites for research and production and directed the enormous construction effort in the states of New Mexico, Tennessee and Washington.

Because of the secrecy associated with the project, a special Manhattan Engineer District Military Police unit was located at Kirtland Field to guard facilities used to load Los Alamos assembled ordnance and tests shapes on aircraft.

On the morning of July 16, 1945, two B-29 Superfortress observation planes set out from Kirtland Field to monitor the first atomic bomb detonation at the Trinity Site. The pilots had instructions to be at least fifteen miles west of the detonation point. In this same time frame, supporting components for the nuclear bombs to be deployed in the Pacific were being shipped piecemeal to Tinian. Components of "Little Boy" were driven from Los Alamos to Kirtland Field and then flown to San Francisco for loading onto a cruiser, USS *Indianapolis*, bound for Tinian. After the successful Trinity detonation, a plutonium core and its initiator were driven to Albuquerque. They left Kirtland Field on July 26 and were flown by C-54 Skymaster to Tinian, where they arrived on July 28 and became part of the "Fat Man" bomb.

Sandia Base emerged in 1946 from the Old Army Air Field that was located on Oxnard Field to become a principal nuclear weapons installation of the United States. Atomic weapons research, development, design, testing and training was conducted on the base under various branches of the U.S. government.

Sandia Laboratory, often called "Sandia," was established on Sandia Base to support the Atomic Energy Commission and later Department of Energy (DOE). Initially, the laboratory was operated as Z-Division of the Los Alamos Laboratory by the University of California from 1945 until 1949. In 1948, President Harry S Truman asked Western Electric, a subsidiary of American Telephone and Telegraph (AT&T), to assume the operation as an "opportunity to render an exceptional service in the national interest." Sandia Corporation, a wholly owned subsidiary of AT&T Corporation, managed and operated the laboratory until October 1993. Congress designated the expanded Sandia Laboratory as Sandia National Laboratories (SNL) in 1979. Starting in October 1993, SNL was managed and operated by Sandia Corporation, a wholly owned subsidiary of Lockheed Martin. As of May 2017, SNL is managed by National Technology and Engineering Solutions of Sandia, a wholly owned subsidiary of Honeywell International.

From 1946 to 1972, Sandia Base had a military component that was an air force function, not joint service. The military operations at Sandia Base were operated by the Air Force Special Weapons Center (AFSWC). Starting in 1952, the AFSWC would track development of new atomic weapons for deployment by the USAF and perform the drop tests on new weapon designs. The Air Force Weapons Laboratory emerged on the base in the 1960s.

Another base was also created to support the Manhattan Project: Manzano Base. The U.S. government needed sites to store nuclear weapons as part of the nation's stockpile. Portions of America's nuclear stockpile were stored in the Manzano Mountain, which was initially operated by the U.S. Air Force. *Manzano* is the Spanish word for apple. Apple trees, not native to the United States, were found in the east side of the mountains. Construction of Manzano Base began in 1947, and the facility became operational in 1950. Construction crews carved out tunnels and blast-proof underground steel vaults to protect the small stockpile of atomic weapons. Components of the weapons were stored without plutonium, in reinforced concrete and steel bunkers throughout the mountain. Plutonium was stored in secure chambers elsewhere in the mountain. The mountain was surrounded with a barbed, electrified, double-fence line. The fences and concrete bunker entrances to the tunnels are visible.

## Kirtland Air Force Base
2000 Wyoming Boulevard SE
Albuquerque, NM 87117

Kirtland Air Force Base (KAFB) was established on January 13, 1948. It grew out of activities at Kirtland Field, Sandia Base and Manzano Base. Organizations sponsoring activities at Sandia Base and Manzano Base became tenants on KAFB. The transfer of the activities on the old Oxnard Field to Sandia Base—which became home to Sandia Laboratories, AFSWP and the AFSWC—reenergized the base into becoming the main facility for the development of new nuclear weapons designs and the integration of these new weapons onto operational equipment and USAF aircraft. Adjacent Kirtland Field had become a flight test center during nuclear weapons development. As many as twenty thousand people have been employed by different government agencies on KAFB at different times.

## KAFB Access
2000 Wyoming Boulevard SE
Albuquerque, NM 87117
https://www.kirtland.af.mil

Work at Los Alamos, Sandia Laboratories and many air force organizations is still secret in our nation's interest, and it is beyond the scope of this book to do anything but introduce some interesting projects that can be discussed in open literature. Because the activities are on KAFB, visitors can have a difficult time visiting some of these interesting and historic sites. For access, the public affairs office of KAFB must be consulted first. The listing for KAFB provides useful information for inquiries.

## Air Force Special Weapons Center
2000 Wyoming Boulevard SE
Albuquerque, NM 87117
https://www.kirtland.af.mil

The U.S. government decided to create specialized organizations dealing with atomic and other unconventional weapons. During the 1950s, the AFSWC participated in atmospheric nuclear tests in Nevada and the far Pacific. Scientific capabilities were developed at KAFB to evaluate the effects of the explosions. Biophysicists flew through nuclear clouds to assess radiation hazards. Physicists used sounding rockets to study the effects of high-altitude nuclear explosions on the atmosphere and existing radiation belts.

## Air Force Weapons Laboratory
2000 Wyoming Boulevard SE
Albuquerque, NM 87117
https://www.kirtland.af.mil

The United States had signed the Nuclear Test Ban Treaty in 1963, which prohibited further atmospheric testing. Therefore, weapons vulnerability evaluations were forced to focus on nuclear weapons effects simulations. In response to the test ban treaty, the AFSWC evolved into the Air Force Weapons Laboratory (AFWL). This laboratory was responsible for researching nuclear weapons and assessing the vulnerability of U.S. weapons systems to nuclear attack. The AFWL's original mission was to explore the military uses of nuclear power, weapons and support equipment, with emphasis on reducing the vulnerability of U.S. systems to nuclear weapons effects. Four tasks stood out: (1) studying nuclear weapons effects through simulation testing; (2) ensuring the compatibility of nuclear weapons with USAF delivery systems; (3) providing advanced nuclear weapons delivery techniques; and (4) investigating nuclear power concepts.

## ATLAS-I Facility
2000 Wyoming Boulevard SE
Albuquerque, NM 87117
https://www.kirtland.af.mil

Throughout the 1960s, AFWL scientists built facilities to simulate the radiation effects of nuclear attacks such as transient radiation, X-rays and electromagnetic pulse. One major effort during this period was to build a

KAFB trestle at the end of construction phase. *Courtesy of U.S. Air Force.*

facility to evaluate nuclear weapons effects on full-size USAF planes. The ATLAS-I (better known as Trestle), the largest simulation facility ever built, was completed on the east side of KAFB during the late 1970s.

The trestle was built out of timber beams *without any metal fasteners*. This important design feature was to make it possible to radiate the entire plane without electromagnetic interference from metal in the support structure. The structure was large enough to hold a B-52 plane such that comprehensive radiation effects on critical U.S. aircraft could be evaluated. This goal was achieved.

AFWL also made important contributions throughout the decade to improve nuclear system delivery techniques related to aircraft, air-to-ground missiles and intercontinental ballistic missiles.

## Sandia National Laboratories

1611 Innovation Parkway SE
Albuquerque, NM 87123
505-284-3626 | www.sandia.gov

Sandia's primary mission includes maintaining the reliability and surety of nuclear weapon systems, conducting research and development in arms control and nonproliferation technologies and investigating methods for the disposal of the United States' nuclear weapons program's hazardous waste. Other missions include research and development in energy and environmental programs, as well as the surety of critical national infrastructures.

Once Sandia Laboratory was established in 1949, there was confusion as to the roles of the two laboratories located in the state. The overriding activities of the Los Alamos and Sandia laboratories in New Mexico could be summarized as such: Los Alamos would build the "physics package" of a new weapon, and Sandia Laboratory would put the weapon in a case and install firing, fuzing, timing and safety systems and the necessary electromechanical elements. After a weapon was designed, it was essential to successfully marry nuclear weapon hardware with U.S. Air Force planes.

President John F. Kennedy visited Sandia National Laboratories in 1962. Sandia had helped develop Vela satellites to detect special rays that are signatures of nuclear tests. Vela satellites were developed to detect space or

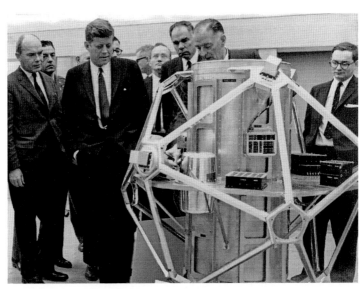

Photograph of President John F. Kennedy visiting Sandia National Laboratories in 1962. *Courtesy of Sandia National Laboratories.*

atmospheric nuclear testing and verify compliance with the Limited Test Ban Treaty of 1963 and, later, the Threshold Test Ban Treaty of 1974. The program provided a hands-off sensor system for space monitoring of and detection of nuclear bursts. Sandia worked closely with Los Alamos National Laboratory (LANL) scientists on the Vela. LANL developed most of the sensors, while Sandia designed the optical sensors and handled the data processing tasks. It has been common that the two laboratories work together on many DOE-related programs.

## Sandia Research Facility Cleanroom
1611 Innovation Parkway SE
Albuquerque, NM 87123
505-284-3626 | www.sandia.gov

As an example of some of Sandia's nonnuclear activities, the modern cleanroom was invented by American physicist Willis Whitfield, who was an employee of Sandia Laboratories in 1960. A cleanroom is a facility ordinarily utilized as part of specialized industrial production or scientific research that includes the manufacture of pharmaceutical items or microprocessors. Cleanrooms are designed to maintain extremely low levels of particulates, such as dust, airborne organisms or vaporized particles.

The importance of the invention is that the integrated circuit manufacturers in Silicon Valley are dependent on cleanrooms for the production of their products. Within a few years of its invention in the 1960s, Whitfield's modern cleanroom had generated more than $50 billion in sales worldwide.

Sandia National Laboratories cleanroom. *Courtesy of Sandia National Laboratories.*

## National Solar Thermal Test Facility
1611 Innovation Parkway SE
Albuquerque, NM 87123
505-844-0964 | www.sandia.gov

As another example of Sandia's diversity in research, the DOE authorized Sandia National Laboratories to construct a solar tower, which has become the National Solar Thermal Test Facility (NSTTF). This is the only test facility of this type in the United States.

The NSTTF's primary goal is to provide experimental engineering data for the design, construction and operation of unique components and systems in proposed solar thermal electrical plants planned for large-scale power generation. The site was built and instrumented to provide test facilities for a variety of solar and non-solar applications.

The facility can provide capabilities to investigate the thermophysical properties of materials in concentrated sunlight, simulations of thermal effects of nuclear explosions on materials and components and performances and failure thresholds of high-temperature ceramic and refractory materials.

Sandia National Laboratories solar tower. *Courtesy of Sandia National Laboratories.*

The facility consists of a heliostat field, which has 218 individual heliostats. Each heliostat has two motors to control azimuth and elevation and can be synchronized with the others to focus and concentrate solar energy on a small area on the solar tower. The facility can achieve concentration of solar energy to represent about four hundred suns on a small area. The tower is a two-hundred-foot-high concrete structure that supports testing of focused solar energy at three locations. The tower has a high-capacity crane for lifting experiments and systems to remove heat from experiments when necessary.

# MUSEUMS, LIBRARIES AND ETHNIC CENTERS

**A** sign of a growing and mature city is the presence of interesting museums and meaningful libraries. Of the museums listed here, three are somewhat traditional in that they deal with the community and its past. The fourth is unique because it deals with the many things that occurred in Albuquerque during the growth of the atomic age. Six public libraries and the university library are briefly discussed to highlight the organizations and contributions of those facilities.

The National Museum of Nuclear Science and History was started on KAFB in 1969 by personnel from the U.S. Air Force and SNL. These two groups wanted to tell the story of the base and the development of nuclear weapons, and they created a museum on the base. It was originally named Sandia Atomic Museum, and later the name was changed to National Atomic Museum. In 1985, the U.S. Department of Energy (DOE) became responsible for the museum. In 1991, the museum received a charter as a national museum, and its mission expanded to include aspects of nuclear science and history beyond the manufacturing of nuclear weapons. Funding for the museum became a problem, and in 1992, the National Atomic Museum Foundation (NAMF) was created to act as a supporting organization. NAMF collects revenues from admissions, memberships, grants, summer camps, rentals and museum store proceeds. The DOE transferred the museum operation to SNL in 1995. In 2005, NAMF became responsible for the operation of the museum.

One of the distinguishing features of Albuquerque is its diversity and the pride that is shown in celebrating this fact. Two ethnic centers provide access to important cultures that have helped form and define the community we live in. The National Hispanic Cultural Center (NHCC) is dedicated to preserving, promoting and advancing Hispanic culture, arts and humanities. The Indian Pueblo Cultural Center is dedicated to the preservation and perpetuation of Pueblo Indian culture, history and art. The African American community is developing a museum and cultural center that is designed to increase awareness and understanding of the contributions of people of African descent to New Mexico and the Southwest. Currently, the Alice K. Hoppes African American Pavilion is dedicated to an individual who pioneered this desire.

## Albuquerque Museum
2000 Mountain Road NW
Albuquerque, NM 87104
505-243-7255 | www.albuqueruqemuseum.com

The Albuquerque Museum is dedicated to preserving the art of the American Southwest and the history of Albuquerque and the Middle Rio Grande Valley of New Mexico. The history collection at the museum was initiated with a major donation of about one thousand objects assembled by the Albuquerque Historical Society between the 1940s and 1960s. The City of Albuquerque–supported museum features more than four hundred years of Albuquerque history with permanent installations and special short-term displays. The museum has a rich collection of historic photographs that document Albuquerque, its people,

Entrance to Albuquerque Museum. *Norman Falk, photographer.*

architecture, businesses, urban landscape and depictions of daily life and important events.

Archaeological materials have been donated by the Albuquerque High School and the Albuquerque Historical Society. Donated collections highlight the founding of Villa de Alburquerque, Spanish Colonial and Mexican history, sixteenth- to twentieth-century agriculture and ranching, records from the Territorial period (1850–1912), objects from the Confederate occupation of Albuquerque (1862), the arrival of the railroad, ballooning, aviation and automobile travel and Route 66.

## New Mexico Museum of Natural History and Science
Mountain Road NW
Albuquerque, NM 87104
505-252-6869 | http://nmnaturalhistory.org

The New Mexico Museum of Natural History and Science showcases New Mexico's prehistoric life as it was millions of years ago. Visitors enter the Mesozoic era of the largest of lizards, welcomed by life-size New Mexico dinosaurs cast in bronze before a face-to-face encounter with a Tyrannosaurus rex in full attack mode. The T. rex is a replica of a nearly complete skeleton found in South Dakota. Fossils of the Tyrannosaurus's relatives have been discovered all over New Mexico. The State of New Mexico–supported museum takes a fun approach to informal science education that visitors enjoy in permanent exhibitions,

Entrance to New Mexico Museum of Natural History and Science. *Courtesy of New Mexico Museum of Natural History and Science.*

including an active walk-through volcano, a realistic ice age cave, a living forest and a marine aquarium.

Ever changing are presentations in the Planetarium and Extreme Screen DynaTheater, and visitors can do their own thing and touch everything on exhibit. The theater features the world's first 2D/3D system, allowing both 2D and 3D films to be shown. A planetarium is located in the museum that offers three different shows about space, the night sky and a variety of astronomy topics. One of the regular shows is an introduction to the stars in the heavens and our solar system. A digital system projects onto a domed theater for an immersive experience.

## Maxwell Museum of Anthropology

500 University Boulevard NE
Albuquerque, NM 87131
505-277-4405 | http://maxwellmuseum.unm.edu

The Maxwell Museum of Anthropology is free and open to all. The museum is sponsored by the University of New Mexico and enhances the university's mission of education, research and public service. The mission of the museum is to increase knowledge and understanding of the human cultural experience across space and time. The archaeological exhibit provides evidences of groups from the prehistoric American Southwest. Museum collections span the globe, with objects representing multiple subfields of anthropology along with photo and document archives. The museum has many learning programs, including exhibits and lectures.

The museum has five exhibit areas that host permanent and changing exhibits that express the human cultural experience. The permanent "Ancestors" exhibit traces human evolution over 4 million years. The permanent "People of the Southwest" exhibit depicts eleven thousand years of the cultural heritage of the American Southwest and features artifacts from Mimbres, Ancestral Puebloan and Puebloan cultures. Changing exhibits, which feature artifacts from the extensive museum collection as well as traveling exhibits, are provided at other galleries and spaces.

Maxwell Museum of Anthropology. *Courtesy of Maxwell Museum of Anthropology.*

## National Museum of Nuclear Science and History
601 Eubank Boulevard SE
Albuquerque, NM 87123
505-245-2137 https://www.nuclearmuseum.org

The National Museum of Nuclear Science and History is a repository of nuclear science information and has a mission to serve as America's resource for nuclear history and science. The museum presents exhibits and quality educational programs that convey the diversity of individuals and events that shape the historical and technical content of the nuclear age.

Permanent exhibits include an interactive display that introduces the individuals who pioneered the study of the atom. Displays of World War II activities leading to the creation and use of the atomic bomb are discussed. Later Cold War developments in the conflict between the United States and Russia are explained. Nuclear energy developments for nonmilitary applications are introduced and discussed, as are explanations of applications of nuclear medicine, uses of atomic energy for energy production and insights into nuclear waste transportation features.

Entrance to National Museum of Nuclear Science and History. *Courtesy of New Mexico National Museum of Nuclear Science and History.*

The September 2001 terror attacks caused increased security at KAFB, and the public access to the museum was restricted. The museum was temporarily relocated to a building in Old Town. In 2005, NAMF was successful in getting the DOE to donate twelve acres of land at the corner of Eubank and Southern Boulevards for the establishment of a permanent museum facility that provided outdoor space for exhibits of military aircraft, missiles, vehicles and the sail of a nuclear submarine. The new museum opened in 2009.

### Special Collections Library
423 Central Avenue NE
Albuquerque, NM 87108
505-848-1376

The Special Collections Library houses research collections on Albuquerque history and New Mexico history and culture. The 1925 Pueblo/Spanish Revival–style building is a registered Albuquerque landmark in the historic Huning Highlands neighborhood. Research collections are available for in-house use only. The Special Collections Library was separated from the Main Library in 1978 when the main library moved downtown.

The collections include scholarly publications on history, anthropology, archaeology, religion, language and art in Albuquerque and the region. Popular topics about ghosts and aliens are also included. The library is a great resource for researching the pre-Entrada, Spanish Colonial, Mexican, Territorial and Statehood eras of New Mexico and the Southwest. The library maintains an excellent collection of postcards that have been published during the twentieth century.

## Genealogy Library
501 Copper Avenue NW
Albuquerque, NM 87102
505-768-5131

The Genealogy Center's resources include:

- databases from home (Fold3, military records; Heritage Quest, family and local history books; Newspaper ARCHIVE, historic newspapers; World Vital Records; and Sanborn Digital Maps)
- databases from your branch library (Ancestry Library Edition)
- databases from your Genealogy Center (American Ancestors; locally created databases including Albuquerque obituaries, Albuquerque high school yearbooks, New Mexico death certificates from 1912 to 1950, books and CD databases from throughout the United States and the world and much more)

## Ernie Pyle Library
900 Girard Boulevard SE
Albuquerque, NM 87106
505-256-2065

The Ernie Pyle house has been converted into a library, called the Ernie Pyle Library, and is a monument to the man. The house is listed in the National Register of Historic Places, as a U.S. National Historic Landmark, in the New Mexico State Register of Cultural Properties and as an Albuquerque Historic Landmark. The house was built in 1940 and was the home of famed war correspondent Ernie Pyle from that time until his untimely death in 1945. It now serves as a branch of the Albuquerque Bernalillo

Ernie Pyle Library. *Historic Albuquerque Inc., Nancy Tucker Collection.*

County Library System and contains Pyle memorabilia. This building was designated as the first branch for the library system in 1947.

Pyle sometimes mentioned the "little white house and picket fence" back in Albuquerque. They have been preserved. His dog, Cheeta, has a grave marker on the property.

Pyle's dispatches from military theaters overseas during World War II focused on the war through the experiences of front-line infantry soldiers. Harry Truman wrote, "No man in this war has so well told the story of the American fighting man as American fighting men wanted it told." Pyle was the recipient of the Pulitzer Prize for distinguished war correspondence in 1944. He was killed by enemy fire on the island of Iejima during the Battle of Okinawa in 1945.

## Erna Ferguson Library
3401 Monroe Street NE
Albuquerque, NM 87110
505-888-8100

The Erna Fergusson Library was opened in 1966. The library was named for Erna Fergusson, who was a writer, historian and storyteller who documented the culture and history of New Mexico for more than forty years.

Fergusson was the eldest child of Harvey Butler Fergusson, a prominent lawyer, and Clara Mary Huning, who was the eldest daughter of Franz Huning, one of the three founders of New Town Albuquerque. She went through the Albuquerque schools and graduated from Central High School in 1906. She graduated from UNM in 1912 with a pedagogy degree. She later got a master's in history at Columbia University in New York and received an honorary Doctorate of Letters from UNM in 1943.

Fergusson was depicted as a New Mexico writer in the 1930s, honing the two techniques of oral interview and conversational prose. She published her first book, *Dancing Gods*, in 1931, which was about Indian ceremonials, and it was very successful. In 1934, she published a Mexican cookbook. She was a reporter for the *Albuquerque Herald* in the late 1920s and published many articles about New Mexico.

## Tony Hillerman Library

8205 Apache Avenue NE
Albuquerque, NM 87110
505-291-6264

The Tony Hillerman Library was named for Hillerman in 2008. Hillerman was a noted American author of detective novels and nonfiction works that emphasized locations and characters from the Navajo tribal police.

Hillerman was born and raised in Oklahoma. He was a decorated combat veteran of World War II, from which he received the Silver Star, the Bronze Star and a Purple Heart. After studying at the University of Oklahoma, he moved to Santa Fe in 1952 and worked as a journalist. He moved his family to Albuquerque in 1966 and earned a master's degree from the UNM. He taught journalism at UNM from 1966 to 1987. He also started writing books during this period. He wrote more than thirty books, among them a memoir and books about the Southwest. Of this total, eighteen were in his Navajo tribal police series.

Hillerman's novel *Skinwalkers* won the 1988 Anthony Award for Best Novel, and his short story collection *The Mysterious West* won the 1995 Anthony Award in the "Best Anthology/Short Story Collection" category. He won the Best Critical or Biographical Award in the 2002 Anthony Awards competition for his memoir, *Seldom Disappointed*.

## Rudolfo Anaya Library
7704 Second Street NW
Albuquerque, NM 87107
505-897-8823

The Rudolfo Anaya North Valley Library was named for Rudolfo in March 2018. Rudolfo Anaya is best known for his 1972 novel, *Bless Me, Ultima*, and is considered as one of the founders of the canon of contemporary Chicano literature.

He was raised in Santa Rosa, New Mexico. His father was a vaquero from a family of cattle workers and sheepherders, and his mother's family was composed of farmers from the Pecos Valley. The family moved to Albuquerque when he was in the eighth grade, and he graduated from Albuquerque High School in 1956. He earned a Bachelor of Arts in English and American literature from UNM in 1963 and later earned two master's degrees, one for English in 1968 and the other for guidance and counseling in 1972. He worked as a high school English teacher in Albuquerque public schools from 1963 to 1968. He began writing *Bless Me, Ultima* in 1963 and struggled to get it published. The book went on to sell more than 300,000 copies in twenty-one printings. He then joined the English faculty at UNM and taught there until his retirement in 1993. He published six books for Warner: *Alburquerque, Zia Summer, Rio Grande Fall, Jalamanta: A Message from the Dessert, Shaman Winter* and *The Anaya Reader*.

## Zimmerman Library
1900 Roma Avenue NE
Albuquerque, NM 87106

The Zimmerman Library at UNM is the main library for the university. It was designed by John Gaw Meem in 1936 and opened on April 1, 1938. The building was named after late UNM president James F. Zimmerman, who served as president from 1927 to 1944.

The building was one of the Public Works Administration (PWA) projects on the UNM campus and was funded under the Works Progress Administration (WPA). The Spanish Pueblo–style structure is highlighted by a central nine-story book tower of reinforced concrete, relieved by vertical rows of windows. The two-story main structure was flanked by

Zimmerman Library. *Historic Albuquerque Inc., Nancy Tucker Collection.*

flat-roofed wings projecting to the north, south, east and west. A traditional portal runs along the main west façade. The interior of the building is emphasized by the work of local craftspeople, including punched-in light fixtures, elaborate wood carving and hand-made furniture. The building was remodeled and upgraded in 1965, 1974 and 2001 to accommodate the growing needs of a rapidly expanding and maturing university. The building is in the National Register of Historic Places.

UNM's Zimmerman Library is highlighted because of its Center for Southwest Research (CSWR), which houses collections that include publications, government documents, maps and journal databases documenting New Mexico and the Southwest, with emphasis on Route 66. In addition to books, the library contains numerous periodicals, audio tapes and videos that document the communities and businesses along the route of US 66 from Tucumcari in the east to Gallup in the west, as well as coverage of the important El Camino Real and Santa Fe Trail contributions to our history.

## National Hispanic Cultural Center
1701 Fourth Street SW
Albuquerque, NM 87102
505-246-2261 | http://www.nhccnm.org

The NHCC's twenty-acre campus is located along the Rio Grande in Albuquerque, New Mexico. The NHCC is home to three theaters, an art museum, a library, a genealogy center, a Spanish-language resource center and two restaurants. A distinct feature is that the NHCC has the largest concave fresco in North America.

The NHCC, which was opened in 2000, sits within the Barelas neighborhood, a traditionally Hispanic neighborhood that has historically been a crossroads for New Mexico's people. The architectural design of the NHCC recalls styles from Spain, Mesoamerica and early New Mexico. The NHCC is part of the State of New Mexico's Department of Cultural Affairs. It is supported through the National Hispanic Cultural Center Foundation.

National Hispanic Cultural Center. *Courtesy of National Hispanic Cultural Center.*

## Indian Pueblo Cultural Center

2401 Twelfth Street NW
Albuquerque, NM 87104
505-843-7270 | www.indianpueblo.org

The Indian Pueblo Cultural Center is a nonprofit that opened in August 1976 to showcase the history and accomplishments of the Pueblo people, from the pre-Columbian era to current time. The center is owned and operated by 19 Indian Pueblos of New Mexico.

The center includes a ten-thousand-square-foot museum of the authentic history and artifacts of traditional Pueblo cultures and their contemporary art. A permanent exhibit titled "We Are of This Place: The Pueblo Story" opened on April 2, 2016, and highlights the creativity and adaptation that made possible the survival, diversity and achievements of each of the 19 Pueblos. The center also includes a small, changing exhibit that highlights the work of living traditional and contemporary artists. Traditional Indian dances and artist demonstrations are open to the public on Saturday and Sunday.

Indian Pueblo Cultural Center. *Courtesy of Indian Pueblo Cultural Center.*

## Alice K. Hoppes African American Pavilion

300 San Pedro NE
Albuquerque, NM 87108
505-222-9700 | http://www.exponm.com/p/246

The Alice K. Hoppes African American Pavilion was dedicated at Expo New Mexico in Albuquerque in 2004 to honor an individual who accomplished much for the African American community. Alice lived a life that produced children and grandchildren while achieving many professional accomplishments for the community. She participated in civil rights marches and promotion of African American issues. She headed the state Office of African American Affairs. One of her accomplishments was getting Martin Luther King Jr.'s birthday made a state holiday. She was president of the National Association for the Advancement of Colored People (NAACP) in New Mexico. The New Mexico chapter of the NAACP was started in 1915 after another civil rights group, the Independent Society of New Mexico, decided to affiliate with the NAACP in order to get involved in a national organization. The parent group got started in 1909.

African American Pavilion. *Norman Falk, photographer.*

# RECREATION AND ENTERTAINMENT

Albuquerque is known for several recreational and entertainment events that have histories that started more than fifty years ago. Three are featured in this document: ballooning, Sandia Peak Tramway and automobile racing by the Unser family at the Indianapolis Motor Speedway and Pike's Peak. In addition, four theaters and performing arts centers are highlighted.

Albuquerque is known for its hot-air ballooning. It hosts the Albuquerque International Balloon Fiesta each year, which attracts hundreds of thousands of people. What is less well known is that ballooning started in Albuquerque as early as 1882. Park Van Tassel was living in Albuquerque and was operating the Elite Saloon. Van Tassel was paid to put on a balloon exhibition and launch a manned balloon from an empty lot near Second Street and Gold Avenue on July 4, 1882. He bought a balloon made from cattle intestines in California and transported it to Albuquerque. The balloon was to be filled with coal gas, which was collected from local residents.

On the morning of the Fourth, Albuquerque was flooded by people arriving in wagons, on horseback or burro and on foot. The launch was scheduled for 10:00 a.m. A number of complications arose, and a partially filled balloon was finally scheduled to launch at 7:00 p.m. The first attempt at launching failed with Van Tassel and a passenger, a local reporter. The passenger stepped out, and Van Tassel tossed a sandbag over the side. The balloon began a slow ascent and reached a

The balloon ascension of Park Van Tassel on Second Street between Railroad and Gold, July 4, 1882. *Albuquerque Museum, 1978.050.036, courtesy of University of New Mexico Library.*

total altitude of 14,207 feet, at which time Van Tassel opened a valve and there was a rapid descent. Van Tassel threw many items overboard to slow his descent and finally landed in a cornfield near Railroad Avenue and Rio Grande Boulevard, which was near the Territorial Fairgrounds. Thus, Albuquerque's balloon activities were started in the nineteenth century.

The Sandia Peak Tramway has provided a spectacular view of the west side of the Sandia Mountains and all of the land to the west since 1966. More than 11 million passengers have taken the fifteen-minute ride to the top of the mountain just below the peak. The tram is one of the most popular tourist attractions in Central New Mexico. The scenery steals the show. The tram celebrated its fiftieth anniversary in May 2016.

Automobile racing at Indianapolis Speedway has been called the greatest spectacle in racing. Three descendants of the Louis Unser family from Albuquerque have distinguished themselves at the speedway. Bobby won three titles, in 1968, 1975 and 1981. Younger brother Al won four titles, in 1970, 1971, 1978 and 1987, where he was the oldest driver to win the famed race. Al's son, Al Jr., won in 1992 and 1994. Thus, the family have spread out wins over a quarter of a century. The family drivers were also multiple winners at the Pike's Peak International Hill Climb. They have a museum commemorating these outstanding performances. Unser Boulevard is a major arterial thoroughfare in west Albuquerque.

## International Balloon Fiesta Museum

9201 Balloon Museum Drive NE
Albuquerque, NM 87113
505-768-6020 | https://www.balloonmuseum.com

The Albuquerque Balloon Fiesta began in 1972 as the highlight of a fiftieth-birthday celebration for 770 KOB Radio, an AM station at 770kHz. The manager of the radio station asked Sid Cutter, owner of Cutter Flying Service and the first person to own a hot-air balloon in New Mexico, if KOB could use his new hot-air balloon as part of the festivities. The two began discussing ballooning and decided to invite as many balloonists as possible to highlight the celebration. The first fiesta ended up with thirteen

Hot-air balloons in flight at Balloon Fiesta. *Roger Zimmerman Collection.*

Anderson Abruzzo Albuquerque International Balloon Museum. *Courtesy of Anderson Abruzzo Albuquerque International Balloon Museum.*

balloons on April 8, 1972. Balloonists from Arizona, California, Iowa, Michigan, Minnesota, Nevada and Texas took part. The first event was located in the parking lot of the Coronado Center Shopping Mall with ten thousand people present.

The organizers of the event scheduled some races, and this seemed to be an attractive activity for the balloonists. The organizing committee tried some experiments in scheduling times of event and format for the next three years. The committee finally decided on October as the best time for the fiestas. Now the Balloon Fiesta is a nine-day event in the first two weekends in October.

The Balloon Fiesta grew each year for decades, and today it is the largest balloon convention in the world. The number of registered balloons reached a peak of 1,019 in 2000, prompting the Balloon Fiesta Board to limit the number to 750 starting in 2001, citing a desire for "quality over quantity." The limit was changed to 600 in 2009 citing recent growth in the city and a loss of landing zones. Now the balloon fiesta and has more than 500 hot-air balloons each year. On any given day during the festival, up to 100,000 spectators may be on the launch field, where they are provided the rare opportunity to observe inflation and takeoff procedures.

The Anderson Abruzzo Albuquerque International Balloon Museum provides a gateway to balloon-related exploration, discovery and achievement. The museum provides information about the history, science, sport and art of ballooning. One feature of the museum are the displays and information explaining how ballooning got started in 1783 and has progressed since. The museum provides many educational programs, including interactive exhibitions.

The museum, which was opened in 2005, was named in honor of Maxie Anderson and Ben Abruzzo, both from Albuquerque, who, along with Larry Newman, were part of a three-person team that successfully flew across the Atlantic Ocean for the first time in 1978.

## Sandia Peak Tramway
30 Tramway Road NE
Albuquerque, NM 87112
505-856-7325 | www.sandiapeak.com

Passengers taking the tramway from the base to the top ascend four thousand feet in about fifteen minutes, gliding along the western face of the rugged Sandia Mountains. The granite rock face forms the bulk of the exposed surface that had risen miles from its original home. The rugged surface contains spires, cliffs, pinnacles and deep canyons. In fertile areas on the slope, there are many different types of trees, including aspens, pines, scrub oaks, Douglas firs and blue spruces. Tram riders may see an eagle or a mule deer or perhaps a black bear or coyote as they look out the windows of the cable car into the canyons and ridges.

The Sandia Peak Tram is 2.7 miles in length. A continuous

Sandia Peak Tramway in route to the top. *Roger Zimmerman Collection.*

cable goes from the bottom to the top and returns. Two tram cars are attached to the cable, and the average speed is 12.0 miles per hour. The weight of the downhill cable helps to pull the uphill tramcar to the top. The tramcars meet and pass each other midway when they are almost one thousand feet above the ground. Each tramcar is capable of carrying fifty passengers, or ten thousand pounds, up the mountain at a maximum rate of two hundred passengers per hour.

The view to the west includes the Rio Grande, a volcano field on the west slope of Albuquerque and Mount Taylor some one hundred miles away. To the north and west are the Jemez Mountains, which contain an enormous caldera, known as the Valle Grande. To the north and east lies the Sangre de Cristo Mountains and the capital city of Santa Fe. To the south, the Estancia Valley and the Manzano Mountains frame the view.

## Unser Racing Museum

1776 Montaño Road NW
Albuquerque, NM 87107
505-341-1776 | www.unserracingmuseum.com

The Unser Racing Museum is a multidimensional museum experience utilizing modern technologies to educate and immerse the visitor in the exciting world of racing. A guided tour is available to learn about the Unser family history and then explore the museum, seeing and interacting with racing history as it happened. The museum features racing history, cars and memorabilia. The museum has been expanded to include an all-new annex. The annex contains a wide variety of cars, from fully restored antiques to winning pace cars and

racecars. There's also a trophy room filled with thousands of unique items, a complete library spanning the history of racing and original artwork.

A gift shop is available with hundreds of items, so visitors can bring home the perfect gift to remember the visit.

Racecar in front of Unser Racing Museum. *Norman Falk, photographer.*

## Sunshine Theater
120 Central Avenue SW
Albuquerque, NM 87102
505-764-0249 | www.sunshinetheaterlive.com

The Sunshine Theater is the first of early theaters that has survived the test of time. The theater exists in a six-story building in downtown Albuquerque at the intersection of Second Street and Central Avenue. The building was constructed in 1924 to contain offices and a 920-seat movie theater. The theater was designed for stage productions and has a large stage and adjoining dressing rooms. The building is of reinforced concrete construction with a façade of yellow brick. The theater is listed in the National Register of Historical Places.

## KiMo Theater
423 Central Avenue NW
Albuquerque, NM 87102
505-768-3522 | http://www.cabq.gov/culturalservices/kimo

The KiMo Theater was built in 1927 by Oreste Bachechi and his wife, Maria, with a goal of giving a tribute to the Native Americans who had embraced the Bachechi family as part of their own. The theater is

KiMo Theater. Historic Albuquerque Inc. *Ed Boles Collection.*

a three-stepped stucco building with features highlighting native Pueblo architecture and Art Deco skyscrapers. The interior and the exterior incorporate a variety of indigenous motifs and Native American murals. The name for the theater was suggested by Isleta Pueblo governor Pablo Abeita and is loosely translated as "King of the Beasts," after the mountain lions prevalent in the nearby mountains.

The theater went into a phase of decline in the 1970s, and there was a small fire in 1977. The City of Albuquerque purchased the building and has been restoring it since. The restorations were completed in 2000, and now movies and productions can be provided in an auditorium that seats 650. The theater is listed in the National Register of Historical Places.

## Albuquerque Little Theater

224 San Pasquale SW
Albuquerque, NM 87104
505-242-4750 | https://albuquerquelittletheatre.org

In 1930, a group of civic-minded citizens started a local theater group for the purpose of providing live theater entertainment. The group met in the KiMo Theater for its first six years and then was successful in getting the original building as the first structure to be built in Albuquerque as part of the WPA phase of President Franklin Roosevelt's New Deal. Many well-known celebrities have performed in the Little Theater, which has a seating capacity of 480.

## Popejoy Hall

203 Cornell Avenue NE
Albuquerque NM 87106
505-277-8010 | http://www.popejoypresents.com

Tom Popejoy was a native New Mexican who grew up on a ranch east of Raton. He graduated from UNM, and after working in different capacities there, he was appointed president in 1948 and served for twenty years. He oversaw the largest growth period that UNM has ever had. He built classrooms, dormitories, research facilities, the basketball arena, the Pit and a performing arts center. He promised that he would

Popejoy Hall. *Courtesy of University of New Mexico Center for Southwest Research.*

build a performing arts center early in his presidency and finally achieved it in 1966 after he got City of Albuquerque support for the location of the hall on the UNM campus. He retired two years after the University Concert Hall was built, and the regents gave him the choice to have the new basketball arena, "The Pit," or the new performing arts hall named after him; he chose the hall.

The Popejoy Performing Arts Center has hosted touring musicals, lectures, dance performances, live theater and symphony concerts. It hosts 250,000 people per year.

# DISPLAYS AND SPECIAL TREASURES

**A**lbuquerque has many types of displays to celebrate its unique history. One of the special display features is the Petroglyph National Monument on the escarpment on the west mesa. The monument, located within our city limits, provides evidence of our ancient past. The monument is intended as a protection for these lands and sites and also a recreational site where visitors can access these treasures for generations to come.

The entrance to the Albuquerque Museum features a special historical sculpture display that needs some explanation. The display is a collection of life-size sculptures that show the harsh travel conditions of the early Spanish settlers on El Camino Real—it is named *La Jornada*. The bronze sculptures were commissioned by the City of Albuquerque in 1997 to celebrate the 400th anniversary (*Cuarto Centenario*) of Spanish arrival in New Mexico in 1998. The originators of the display wanted to celebrate Oñate's arrival in 1598, bringing Spanish culture to the region and establishing the first capital. As it turned out, Oñate applied harsh measures to get the residents of Acoma Pueblo to accept Spanish rule, and residents of that pueblo still resent the encounter. Supporters of the pueblo made strong protests to the city about honoring Oñate. Years of controversy and compromise brought about a change in the design of the exhibit, which was finally installed in 2005, some seven years late. Instead of having a memorial to Oñate, the exhibit evolved into a magnificent display of a group of Spanish settlers traveling with Oñate over a difficult landscape. The display has a native Mexican guide in a prominent position. The exhibit highlights the trials and tribulations that the early Spanish settlers had to endure for about six months to bring their culture to what was to become the Province of Santa Fe de Nuevo México.

Albuquerque has more than 175 listed parks and many have historical statues and memorials. Tiguex Park has been mentioned. One of the best collections of historical statues exists in and around the Albuquerque Museum. Sixty-three statues are located in the Sculpture Garden within the facility grounds. Plaques, murals and frescos abound in Albuquerque. Two are listed as being representative of the rest.

As a representative example for a memorial, a person, John Braden, is singled out in a memorial fountain because of the feat of heroism that he demonstrated. The fountain is located in Robinson Park, which was established in 1880 as part of the original plat of New Town. Fairview Memorial Park is selected as a representative for discussion because it was started shortly after the railroad arrived and served as a final resting place for many who contributed to Albuquerque's modern history.

There are eighteen historic districts in Bernalillo County identified by the New Mexico Historic Preservation Division. Two are selected as representatives. The Huning Highland Historic District was the city's first subdivision. It was platted by Franz Huning the same month as the coming of the railroad in 1880. A second historic district presented is the Aldo Leopold Neighborhood Historic District. Aldo Leopold, who is considered the father of modern wildlife ecology, spent thirteen productive years in Albuquerque and left his mark on the development of the city and region. His house is part of the historic district, and he has a small forest along the Rio Grande named after him.

Finally, this guide to Albuquerque history reaches an end with the mention of an outstanding life that was lived here. Sister Blandina Segale contributed much to the growth and well-being of the city and has been nominated and is being considered for sainthood in the Catholic Church. Her accomplishments and drive certainly symbolize the spirit that has occurred in the Middle Valley of the Rio Grande.

## Petroglyph National Monument

6001 Unser Boulevard NW
Albuquerque, NM 87120
505-899-0205 | https://www.nps.gov/petr/index.htm

The Petroglyph National Monument protects a variety of cultural and natural resources, including five volcanic cones, hundreds of archaeological sites and an estimated twenty-four thousand images carved by Ancestral Pueblo peoples and early Spanish settlers. The monument is intended as a protection for these lands and sites and also as a recreational site where visitors can access these treasures for generations to come.

The monument has four major sites that visitors can access over a seventeen-mile stretch along Albuquerque's west mesa, which is the volcanic basalt escarpment that dominates the city's western horizon. The western boundary of the monument features the chain of five dormant fissure-type volcanoes that can be seen from downtown Albuquerque.

The Petroglyph National Monument is cooperatively managed by the National Park Service and the City of Albuquerque and is listed in the National Register of Historic Places.

Image at Petroglyph National Monument. *Courtesy of Petroglyph National Monument.*

## *La Jornada*/Cuarto Centenario
### Intersection of Nineteenth Street and Mountain Road NW

The collection of bronze statues at the entrance to the Albuquerque Museum highlights the immigration of early Spanish settlers into New Mexico. The artists, Renaldo Rivera and Betty Sabo, show children, animals and supplies along with soldiers, a priest and ox carts. Animals include cattle, horses, oxen, a sheep, a goat, a donkey, a dog and a pig. The scene is of this group struggling to push the cart up a hill. These statues depict the harsh and dangerous travel through La Jornada at the time when Oñate and his party settled the province of Santa Fe de Nuevo México. It is recalled that Oñate had 130 families in this journey. The display has plaques naming the 600 settlers who came with Oñate.

Controversy has arisen because of the implied presence of Oñate, but the surrounding statues do a marvelous job of illustrating the hardships that a large group of settlers had to endure. The travel conditions were harsh and provided a severe test to the stamina and willpower of the settlers. What would Albuquerque look like today if these settlers hadn't attempted and survived this journey?

Statues of Spanish settlers with Oñate in 1598. *Norman Falk, photographer.*

## Plaque at Central Avenue and Third Street

300 Central Avenue SW

Plaque on wall of building in downtown Albuquerque. *Roger Zimmerman Collection.*

Plaques adorn a number of buildings in Old Town and New Town. There is no protocol that must be followed in either the location or content of a plaque. For private buildings, owners are free to make historical statements as they see fit. Sometimes officials from one of the city departments will approach an owner and offer to place a plaque on a building with the owner's permission. This is usually done where there is some historical significance associated with the building or location. A plaque is attached to a private building at the southwest corner of Central Avenue and Third Street, for example. The building is at the location where the Armijo Hotel stood at one time.

The plaque shows a rendering of a photograph of a parade in the 1800s and describes early life in Albuquerque. Others like this can be found on some of the downtown buildings.

The Alvarado Transportation Center, which is a multimodal transportation hub for city and is located on the lot used by the Alvarado Hotel in railroad days at First Street and Central Avenue, contains a number of historical plaques and markers. Other properties identified in the National Register usually have identifying plaques and contain some historical information.

## Mural on La Hacienda Restaurant

302 San Felipe Street NW
Albuquerque, NM 87104
505-243-3131

Albuquerque abounds with murals depicting history, culture and art. The mural included here describes the founding of Albuquerque in 1706. It is on the plaza side of the La Hacienda Restaurant in Old Town.

## John Braden Memorial Fountain
Robinson Park at Eight Street and Central Avenue NW

The John Braden Memorial Fountain exists in Robinson Park to honor a fallen hero.

There was a parade in Albuquerque on October 16, 1896, celebrating a weeklong Carnival of Sports at the New Mexico Territorial Fairgrounds. Downtown Albuquerque was lit up for the evening parade. There were displays of electric lamps, moving lights and colored torches. Rockets were fired from various parade units. Near the end of the procession was a horse-drawn ammunition wagon loaded with fireworks. Seventy-four-year-old John Braden was driving the wagon. The *Albuquerque Daily Citizen* described the event. Just as the parade turned south on Fifth Street from Copper Avenue, fireworks and sparks flew back into the ammunition wagon and an explosion occurred. Several rockets shot out of the wagon and struck the horses, which became terror-stricken. They dashed away at a dead run as the wagon turned into a mass of flames. Braden stayed on the wagon as the horses turned east on Railroad Avenue, even though his clothes were becoming enveloped in flames. The horse and wagon, with Braden still aboard, finally ran into a fire cart and was stopped. Braden fell from his seat and was surrounded by parade viewers who unsuccessfully tried to save his life. He had demonstrated personal heroism in staying with the burning wagon after the explosion, and this is the reason for the memorial fountain in his honor.

Robinson Park was platted in the 1880s by Colonel Marmon. The park was formed at the point where Railroad Avenue needed to bend north to go toward Old Town. The irregular shape of the land was unsuitable for residential lots, and a park was formed. The park was named after Albert Alonzo Robinson, who was the general superintendent and chief engineer of the Santa Fe Railway. The naming was accomplished in a fundraising contest to develop the park. Supporters of Robinson raised the most funds and earned the naming honor.

Braden memorial in Robinson Park. *Roger Zimmerman Collection.*

## Fairview Memorial Park

700 Yale Boulevard SE
Albuquerque, NM 87106
505-262-1454 | https://www.fairviewmemorialparkabq.com

There are several cemeteries in Albuquerque. There are about six that are open for interments and others that contain centuries-old burial sites. Fairview Memorial Park is selected to represent the many cemeteries that exist. The cemetery was started after the railroad came and symbolizes the tremendous change that occurred at that time. In November 1882, Elias Stover, later first president of the University of New Mexico, informed the board of trade that individuals were burying their friends along the side of a sand hill that was not intended to be a cemetery. The first documented burial was on February 23, 1881. After the letter, a group of individuals got together and formed the Albuquerque Cemetery Association. The burial ground in the sand hills became Fairview Cemetery and later Fairview Memorial Park.

Fairview Memorial Park has evolved with changing times. Family plots emerged in one region. A special area for children who died from disease or were stillborn was set aside and is being developed as the Historic Fairview Cemetery. In 1892, the Jewish Cemetery Association acquired land that became the Congregation Albert Cemetery. The Strong family, longtime caretakers of the park, built a subdivision that included landscaping and mausoleums.

A number of prominent Albuquerqueans who influenced the history of the community are interred at Fairview Memorial Park. These include Clyde Tingley, longtime ex-officio mayor and state governor; Clinton P. Anderson, U.S. congressman, senator and cabinet secretary; Colonel Francisco Perea, U.S. representative during territorial days; Franz Huning, one of three founders of New Albuquerque; Arthur T. Hannett, former New Mexico governor; Steven Schiff, U.S. congressman; Bernard Rodey, general manager to A&P Railroad and member of the Territorial Senate; Ruth Hanna McCormick Simms, U.S. congresswoman; and Edmund G. Ross, territorial governor of New Mexico, who

The prominent grave of Edmund G. Ross, former territorial governor. *Christine Taute, photographer.*

had been a Kansas senator when President Lincoln was assassinated. Ross was recognized for his voting as a senator by President J.F. Kennedy in his book on *Profiles of Courage*.

## Huning Highland Historic District and Spy House
East of Railroad Tracks and on both sides of Central Avenue

The Huning Highland Historic District was added to the National Register of Historic Places in 1978. The residents were store owners and professional people who had come from the Midwest, and the architecture, emphasizing brick, reflected this. Some homes were modest and others elaborate. It served as a neighborhood that welcomed the many tubercular patients who flocked to Albuquerque with the hope of a cure. World War II created a demand for housing; many of the larger homes were divided into apartments, and smaller houses were bought as rental properties.

One house is singled out in this neighborhood, the Spy House, so named because it became the place where national secrets were shared. David Greenglass was a machinist on the Manhattan Project. He was

Spy House in the Huning Highland neighborhood. *Norman Falk, photographer.*

also a brother of Ethel Rosenberg, who along with her husband, Julius, was involved with Soviet espionage work. The Rosenbergs persuaded Greenglass to provide secrets about the atomic bomb with a visitor who would come with a matching half to a Jello box top. The visitor, Harry Gold, showed up at 209 High Street NE with the matching box top, and Greenglass shared the secrets for a $500 payment.

The spy ring was exposed in 1950, and the Rosenbergs were executed for treason. Greenglass and Gold were sentenced to long terms in prison for their espionage activities.

## Aldo Leopold Neighborhood Historic District and Home
135 Fourteenth Street NW
Albuquerque, NM

Aldo Leopold was influential in the development of modern environmental ethics and in the movement for wilderness conservation through emphasis on wildlife management. Leopold was born in Iowa and educated in forestry at Yale University. He went to work for the U.S. Forest Service in Arizona in 1909 and transferred to the Carson National Forest in northern New Mexico in 1911, where he remained until 1924. He married a local girl, Estella, and together they had five children.

Aldo and Estella and their family lived at 135 Fourteenth Street NW, which is now in the Aldo Leopold Neighborhood Historic District. The historic district was listed in 2002 in the National Register of Historic Places. The neighborhood was the first subdivided portion of the four-hundred-acre Franz Huning estate that formed the western boundary of the original townsite of New Albuquerque.

Leopold became a writer for the forest service and wrote the service's first game and fish handbook. He proposed the Gila Wilderness Area, which was to become the first national wilderness area in the Forest Service System. He went from New Mexico to Wisconsin in 1924 to become an associate director of the U.S. Forest Products Laboratory in Madison, Wisconsin. In 1933, he joined the faculty at the University of Wisconsin, where he was appointed as professor of game management in the Agricultural Economics Department in 1933.

In 1918, Leopold served as the secretary of Albuquerque's chamber of commerce. In this capacity, he created what would later become the Rio Grande Valley State Park and promoted what would eventually be the Rio

Aldo Leopold bicycle path sign. *Richard Ruddy, photographer.*

Grande Nature Center. He was instrumental in getting the Middle Rio Grande Conservancy District started.

In 2009, the City of Albuquerque created the Aldo Leopold Forest, which comprises about fifty-three acres of land extending from the north boundary of the nature center to the southeast side of the Montano Bridge across the Rio Grande. Plans for the forest include a naturally surfaced trail that will connect to other trails on both sides of the Rio Grande.

## Sister Blandina Convent
2005 North Plaza NW
Albuquerque, NM 87104
505-243-4628

A transformational event occurred in Old Town in the 1880s. Marc Simmons reported that in 1880, "Father Gasparri invited the Sisters of Charity to come to Old Albuquerque and take over the Church's education program." The Sisters arrived the next year and found to their dismay that their living quarters were still under construction. Father Gasparri had hired workmen to build a two-story adobe convent along the west side of the church. Rain had slowed the work and caused a corner of the walls to collapse. Simmons noted, "A perky young nun, Sister Blandina Segale, a native of Genoa, Italy, made some suggestions to improve progress, and when he saw that she knew what she was talking about, Father Gasparri eagerly exclaimed, 'For God's sake, Sister, please take it in hand.'" The Sister went back to Santa Fe and contacted an Italian stonecutter who was working on the new cathedral, led him to Albuquerque and instructed him to correct the problem. He did and the convent was completed. This became what many people think was the first two-story building in Old Town. It served as a school building as well as a convent for the nuns.

Sister Blandina didn't stop there. She recognized that future growth in the community would occur in New Albuquerque and promptly encouraged the Sisterhood to obtain sixty-four lots, cornering on Sixth Street and New York Avenue (modern Lomas). In 1882, the nuns initiated work on the new St. Vincent Academy for girls and later added a public

Sister Blandina Convent. *Norman Falk, photographer.*

day school. Sister Blandina was the chief architect and construction superintendent of the new facilities. Sister Blandina later became the mother superior of Our Lady of the Angels School, which was located directly behind the convent.

In 1902, the Sisters of Charity built St. Joseph Sanatorium. In 1887, Sister Blandina had negotiated with Jesuits for a parcel of land on the hills on the north side of town to start a hospital. Sister Hyacinth Sullivan, under the watchful eye of Sister Blandina, is given credit for building the first hospital in Albuquerque.

Sister Blandina wrote a book in 1932, *At the End of the Santa Fe Trail*. In 2015, the Roman Catholic Archdiocese of Santa Fe opened the process to canonize Segale. The Vatican is in the final stages of its inquiry into Sister Blandina's heroic virtue.

## City Landmarks, New Mexico Historic Preservation Division, National Register of Historic Places

There are three main organizations that recognize historical buildings in the city: the Landmarks Commission of the City of Albuquerque's Planning Department, the New Mexico Historic Preservation Division and the National Register of Historic Places. This book has only briefly touched on the many historic places and locations that exist in the Albuquerque area. Readers are encouraged to go to these organizations' websites for a wealth of additional information.

The City Landmarks Commission was formed in 1977 and, among other tasks, prepares and adopts guidelines for designating landmarks, historic zones or urban conservation zones. The commission recommends landmarks to be designated by the city council. In 2018, a total of twenty-three city landmarks was identified by the Landmarks Commission.

The New Mexico Historic Preservation Division identifies and records prehistoric and historic places and maintains records essential for community planning and research. Another duty is to administer state and federal preservation laws and assist local governments in locating schools, parks and historic sites. The division nominates historic places to be listed in the National Register of Historic Places and recommends sites to be included in the State Register of Cultural Properties. A listing of buildings, sites, districts and objects is prepared. In 2018, the list for Bernalillo County alone exceeded 240 items.

Finally, it is seen that the New Mexico Historic Preservation Division makes the recommendations for listings in the National Register of Historic Places. For Bernalillo County, there are more than 145 listings in the register.

LANDMARKS COMMISSION OF THE CITY OF ALBUQUERQUE'S PLANNING DEPARTMENT
https://www.cabq.gov/planning/boards-commissions/landmarks-commission/historic-landmarks

NEW MEXICO HISTORIC PRESERVATION DIVISION
http://www.nmhistoricpreservation.org/documents/state-and-national-register.html

NATIONAL REGISTER OF HISTORIC PLACES
https://nationalregisterofhistoricplaces.com/nm/bernalillo/districts.html

# SELECTED BIBLIOGRAPHY

## BOOKS

Alberts, Don. *Balloons to Bombers.* Aviation in Albuquerque, 1882–1945. Albuquerque, NM: Albuquerque Museum, 1987.

Anna, Timothy. *Iturbide, Congress, and Constitutional Monarchy in Mexico, in the Political Economy of Spanish America in the Age of Revolution, 1750–1850.* Edited by Kenneth J. Andrien and Layman L. Johnson. Albuquerque: University of New Mexico Press, 1994.

Archer, Christon. *Fashioning a New Nation, in the Oxford History of Mexico.* Edited by Michael C. Meyer and William H. Beezley. New York: Oxford University Press, 2000.

Archuletta, Phil. T., and Sharyl S. Holden. *Traveling New Mexico: A Guide to the Historical and State Markers.* Santa Fe, NM: Sunstone Press, 2004.

Balcomb, Kenneth. *A Boy's Albuquerque, 1889–1912.* Albuquerque: University of New Mexico Press, 1980.

Biebel, Charles. *Making the Most of It: Public Works in Albuquerque during the Great Depression, 1929–1942.* Albuquerque, NM: Albuquerque Museum, 1986.

Bryan, Howard. *Albuquerque Remembered.* Albuquerque: University of New Mexico Press, 2006.

Doolittle, George. *As I Remember.* Albuquerque, NM: Aiken Printing, 1973.

Fergusson, Erna. *Do You Remember.* Bernalillo County Special Collections Library Archives, Albuquerque, NM, 2002.

Fitzpatrick, George, and Harvey Caplin. *Albuquerque: 100 Years in Pictures.* Albuquerque, NM: Calvin Horn Publisher, 1975.

Gill, Don. *The Stories Behind the Street Names of Albuquerque, Santa Fe and Taos.* Chicago: Bonus Books Inc., 1994.

Hannett, A.T. *Sage Brush Lawyer.* N.p.: Pageant, 1964.

Herr, Richard. "Revolution and the Meanings of Freedom in the Nineteenth Century." In *The Constitution of 1812 and the Spanish Road to Constitutional Monarchy.* Edited by Isser Wolock. Stanford, CA: Stanford University Press, 1996.

Hughes, Dorothy. *Pueblo on the Mesa: The First Fifty Years at UNM.* Albuquerque: University of New Mexico Press, 1939.

Hurt, Mary Darden, and Lillian Dolde. *That's My Bank!: History of Albuquerque National Bank.* N.p.: Starline Press, 1996.

Johnson, Byron, and Sharon Johnson. *Gilded Palaces of Shame.* Albuquerque, NM: Gilded Age Press, 1983.

Kessell, John L. *Pueblos Spaniards and the Kingdom of New Mexico.* Norman: University of Oklahoma Press, 2008.

Knaut, Andrew L. *The Pueblo Revolt of 1680.* Norman: University of Oklahoma Press, 1995.

Melzer, Richard. *Ernie Pyle in the American Southwest.* Santa Fe, NM: Sunstone Press, 1996.

Price, V.B. *A City at the End of the World.* Albuquerque: University of New Mexico Press, 1992.

Roberts, David. *The Pueblo Revolt.* New York: Simon & Schuster, 2004.

Romero, Cynthia, and Arthur Romero. *Albuquerque Trivia.* Conshohocken, PA: Infinity Publishing, 2007.

Sanchez; Joseph P., Robert L. Spude and Art Gomez. *New Mexico: A History.* Norman: University of Oklahoma Press, 2013.

Segale, Sister Blandina. *At the End of the Santa Fe Trail.* N.p.: Colombian Press, 1932. Reprint, 1948.

Simmons, Marc. *Albuquerque: A Narrative History.* Albuquerque: University of New Mexico Press, 1982.

———. *The Last Conquistador: Juan de Oñate and the Settling of the Far Southwest.* Norman: University of Oklahoma Press, 1991.

Weber, David J. *The Spanish Frontier in North America.* New Haven: Yale Press, 1992.

## ARTICLES AND PAMPHLETS

Bail, E.B. "New Mexico–US 66: Albuquerque's Golden Road." *New Mexico Professional Engineer* (July–August 1952).

# SELECTED BIBLIOGRAPHY

Barnhart, Jan Dodson, and Byron Johnson. *An Albuquerque Bibliography*. Albuquerque: University of New Mexico General Library and the Albuquerque Museum, 1980.

*Church Buildings and Land in Old Albuquerque, in Celebration of the Bicentennial of the Present Church Structure, 1793–1993*. Albuquerque, NM: San Felipe Neri Church, 1993.

Davis, Mary, and Michael J. Rock. *Huning Highland Neighborhood Walking Tour*. Albuquerque, NM: Historic Landmarks Survey. Revised in 1996 by Ann and Jim Carson and Janice Sperling, MD.

DeWitt, Susan. *Historic Albuquerque Today: An Overview Survey of Historic Buildings and Districts*. Albuquerque, NM: Historic Landmarks Survey of Albuquerque, 1978.

Drew, Laurel, Howard Henry and Eldon Pierce. *Newspaper Index, Vital Records in the Albuquerque Daily Citizen, Various Years*. Albuquerque, NM: Genealogy Club of Albuquerque, 1996. Special Collections Library, Edith and Central.

Freeman, Patricia. *S.E. Heights Neighborhoods of Albuquerque*. N.p., 1993.

Johnson, Byron. *Old Town Albuquerque, New Mexico: A Guide to Its History and Architecture*. Albuquerque, NM: Albuquerque City, 1980.

Johnson, Byron, and Robert Dauner. *Early Albuquerque: A Photographic History, 1870–1918*. Albuquerque, NM: Albuquerque Journal and the Albuquerque Museum, 1981.

Kammer, David. *Historic and Architectural Resources of Route 66 through New Mexico*. National Register of Historic Places, U.S. Department of the Interior, National Park Service, August 1993.

Kelley, Vincent C. *Albuquerque: Its Mountains, Valley, Water, and Volcanoes*. Socorro, NM: State Bureau of Mines and Mineral Resources, 1969.

Kelley, Vincent C., and Stuart A. Northrop. *Geology of Sandia Mountains and Vicinity*. Socorro, NM: State Bureau of Mines and Mineral Resources, 1975.

Marshall, Michael. *A Cultural Resource and Historic Architectural Survey for the Downtown Albuquerque Transportation and Streetscape Improvement Project*. Cibola Research Report No. 277, City of Albuquerque Project No. 6323, July 2001.

Salmon, Pamela. *The Presbyterian Odyssey, 1908–1996*. Albuquerque, NM: Presbyterian Healthcare Services, 1996.

Sanchez, Joseph P. *The Rio Abajo Frontier, 1540–1692: A History of Early Colonial New Mexico*. Albuquerque Museum, Albuquerque History Monograph Series, 1987.

# SELECTED BIBLIOGRAPHY

Sando, Joe S., and Herman Agoyo. *Po'Pay: Leader of the First American Revolution.* Santa Fe, NM: Clear Light Publishing, 2005.

Sargeant, Kathryn, and Mary Davis. *Shining River Precious Land: An Oral History of Albuquerque's North Valley.* Albuquerque, NM: Albuquerque Museum, 1986, 1995.

Steele, Thomas J., SJ. *Works and Days: A History of San Felipe Neri Church, 1867–1895.* Albuquerque, NM: Albuquerque Museum, 1983.

Woodham, Marion. *A History of Presbyterian Hospital, 1908–1979.* Albuquerque, NM: Presbyterian Hospital Center, 1979.

Zimmerman, Roger. "The Junction of Route 66 and Route 66: A Memorial to New Mexico's Political Past and Albuquerque's Future." *Route 66 New Mexico* (Winter 2017).

## KAFB-RELATED WEBSITES

Air Force Special Weapons Center. https://www.globalsecurity.org/wmd/agency/swc.htm.

Air Force Weapons Laboratory. http://www.liquisearch.com/kirtland_air_force_base/history/cold_war/air_force_weapons_laboratory.

Atomic Energy Commission. https://www.energy.gov/sites/prod/files/AEC%20History.pdf.

KAFB History. https://www.kirtland.af.mil/About-Us/Fact-Sheets/Display/Article/825960/kirtland-afb-history.

Manzano Base. https://www.globalsecurity.org/wmd/facility/manzano.htm.

Sandia Base. https://www.liquisearch.com/sandia_base.

Sandia National Laboratories. https://www.sandia.gov/about/history/index.html.

# INDEX

# INDEX

# INDEX

## W

## Z

# ABOUT THE AUTHOR

Roger Max Zimmerman was born at Rehoboth Mission east of Gallup, New Mexico. His early years were spent at Mariano Lake Trading Post. He has a Navajo name: Navajo Blue Eyes. He attended the Gallup schools and in 2017 was listed as a "Legendary Local" of that community. He graduated from high school at New Mexico Military Institute and enrolled at the University of Colorado, where he received his BS, MS and PhD degrees. He taught civil engineering at the University of Colorado from 1959 to 1964 and at New Mexico State University from 1964 to 1979. He was then employed at Sandia National Laboratories, where he worked on projects associated with the storage of nuclear waste, weapons components testing programs and rocket systems target deployments. He retired in 2000 as a Distinguished Member of the technical staff and did part-time consulting for another eleven years.

Upon retirement, he pursued his personal interest in exploring local history. He authored a book titled *Kitchen's Opera House, Gallup, New Mexico* with initial publication in 2002 and the second edition coming out in 2012. In 2012, he became active in the Albuquerque Historical Society and became president of the organization in 2013; he completed that activity in 2019. He started a source documents activity where primary documents covering New Mexico history are collected and freely made available on the society website. These primary documents relate to historical activities since New Mexico statehood and were selected to help teachers in their instruction of history at the high school level. He is on the society speaker's bureau and has offerings on: "Son of an Indian Trader/Growing up on the Navajo Reservation"; "Rerouting of Route 66 through Tijeras Canyon"; "Albuquerque and the Yazoo"; "Theoretical Texas Boundary in New Mexico"; and "Opera House in Gallup, New Mexico, without Opera Being Sung." He is one of eleven trained guides who provide free downtown walking tours of Albuquerque, New Mexico.